# Jesus Online

## A Creative Look at a Most Creative Life

## Charles O. Morgan Jr.

Fleming H. Revell
A Division of Baker Book House Co
Grand Rapids, Michigan 49516

© 1995 by Charles O. Morgan Jr.

Published by Fleming H. Revell
a division of Baker Book House Company
P.O. Box 6287, Grand Rapids, MI 49516-6287

Printed in the United States of America

**Library of Congress Cataloging-in-Publication Data**

Morgan, Charles O. Jr.
    Jesus Online : a creative look at a most creative life / Charles O. Morgan Jr.
      p.  cm.
    ISBN 0-8007-5553-7
    1. Jesus Christ—Popular works. 2. Jesus Christ—Biography. I. Title.
BT301.2.M66  1995
232.9'01—dc20
[B]                                                                                     95-3047

This book is dedicated
to the One whose life is the central
focus of this book,
and whose book is the central focus of my life

# Contents

# Introduction

The distraught teenager sat across the desk obviously uncomfortable in a law office. Dressed in tattered jeans and T-shirt, the long-haired youngster spoke softly.

"Tell me again how you found the jewels," I said.

"I ran away from home one night last week," he explained, "and was walking along lookin' for stuff on the railroad tracks at 2 A.M. when I see this bag on the tracks. I shined my flashlight on it and opened the bag. There were the jewels—hundreds of them."

"Eric," I told him, "I read about you finding this jewelry in the paper, but I still find it hard to believe. Sure sounds like you stole it."

"I know," he told me. "That's what the cops said when I turned the stuff in the next day. Then they made me take them to the train tracks where I found it. And when we got there and showed them the exact spot, there was lots more jewelry and diamonds all over the tracks and in the rocks."

"No kidding?" I asked.

"I'm not kidding," he said. "The cops started shoving jewels in their pockets and then told me to go sit in the cop car and wait."

I explained to him that under Florida law, if the finder of personal property gives public notice of his find and the rightful owner does not claim the lost property within six months, the finder becomes the owner.

Eric had already turned over the jewels to the police, so we waited anxiously. After six months, no one laid a legitimate claim to these mysterious jewels. We obtained a court order declaring the jewels to be his—both the jewels that he'd first found *and* those pocketed by the police.

This story had a happy ending for Eric DeWilde, a young orphan who had run away from his foster mother only to find a bank bag containing over a million dollars of jewelry—diamond necklaces and over fifty solitaire diamonds, starting at three carats and one sixteen-carat diamond ring! To this day no one knows the source of this cache of diamonds, a strange unsolved mystery in South Florida.

In a spiritual sense, I can identify with Eric. As a youngster I was an orphan spiritually, searching for meaning to life. I wandered on the tracks seeking to know who God was, who I was, and what life was all about.

As the Lord told the prophet Jeremiah, "You will seek me and find me when you seek me with all your heart" (Jer. 29:13 NIV). I sought him and I found him, or rather *he* found *me*. I discovered in him far greater riches than diamonds; his riches would last forever.

I then continued my search. I wanted to find out all I could about the person of Jesus, this most remarkable individual who walked earth's dusty roads 2,000 years ago, this majestic God/man who split time in two.

I began a personal research project about him. Much has been written about him over the centuries, but the only eyewitness accounts are contained in the Bible books of Matthew, Mark, Luke, and John, a small portion from Acts and Revelation, plus the writings of a few historians. All of these accounts combined can be read in perhaps three hours, which is a pittance compared to the volumes written today about movie stars and athletes.

I also discovered that while Jesus lived among men for thirty-three short years, his agenda was far different from the world around him. He didn't distinguish himself in areas to which society usually ascribes significance. During his earthly tenure:

He never wrote a book.
He never married.
He never accumulated wealth.
He never led an army.
He never held public office.
He never joined a club.
He never earned a degree.
He never established credit.
He was never on the best-dressed list.

His neighbors didn't believe he was anything special. To them he was just one of the neighborhood kids. They wondered in disbelief, "You're telling me this young man is the Messiah? You've got to be kidding!" And they voiced their doubts.

- *Doubts about his lineage.* "Why, he is merely Jesus the son of Joseph, whose father and mother we know" (John 6:42). The neighbors knew Jesus' father as a hardworking carpenter, so Jesus obviously wasn't born into aristocracy. Carpenters' sons become carpenters, not kings or messiahs. The neighbors characterized Jesus' family as blue collar, not blue blood.
- *Doubts about his birthplace.* "How could he be [the Messiah]? For we know where this man was born" (John 7:27). How did the neighbors know that Jesus was Bethlehem born? Possibly they had run a background check and discovered his birthplace from the census public records. The tiny village of Bethlehem, although it was the hometown of King David long ago, was now nothing more than a blip. In fact, Bethlehem had suffered a population decline after King Herod ordered that all young males under age two be killed. Thirty years after the infant executions, the young male shortage was especially evident, and among those living, there was none who would be considered "Most Likely to Become the Messiah."
- *Doubts about his hometown.* "Nazareth! Can anything good come from there?" (John 1:46). Philip, one of Jesus' disciples, invited Nathanael, his best friend, to meet Jesus in Nazareth. Nathanael made the crack, "Can anything good come out of Nazareth?" Nathanael's remark reflects the local prejudice against the town— Nathanael was chairman of the "Just Say No to Nazareth" campaign. If Bethlehem was too small to qualify as Messiah's birthplace, Nazareth was too low class to qualify as his hometown. Nazareth was the pits. Nothing good would come from Nazareth, especially a Messiah. Messiah needs a world-class city.
- *Doubts about his education.* "He's never been to our schools" (John 7:15). How do you regard a Messiah wannabe who doesn't come from politically correct social lines or birthplace or hometown? He's already got three counts against him. Only a Harvard education can give him the stature that he's lacking. He must have proper educational credentials, and this young man doesn't have that either.

When Jesus entered the public arena as the long-awaited Messiah, he obviously didn't command the respect of his peers. Nor did he seek it. His life was not self-centered. He didn't seek his own comfort, convenience, or security. Instead, as Leighton Ford wrote in *Transforming Leadership*, "Jesus was born in a borrowed manger, preached from a borrowed boat, entered Jerusalem on a borrowed donkey, ate the Last Supper in a borrowed upper room, died on a borrowed cross, and was buried in a borrowed tomb." He undoubtably could identify with the lyrics of the spiritual: "This world is not my home, I'm just a passin' through. My treasures are laid up somewhere beyond the blue." He was on a mission—a mission to please God, not impress people. According to his disciple John, "He came unto his own, and his own received him not" (John 1:12 KJV). Jesus was rejected by his neighbors, betrayed by his treasurer, and abandoned by his disciples.

In view of all that Jesus Christ did *not* accomplish, why then did his life stop and restart history's calendar—from B.C. to A.D.? Out of ten billion-plus people who have walked this earth, why is Jesus' life the singular standout?

It is with the orientation of asking questions that I have studied the life of Jesus. I have asked myself lots of questions about him—not questions of doubt, but of curiosity. Questions like:

- Why do we know so little about Jesus' childhood?
- Did Jesus work? Or worry? Or sneeze?
- How could he love his enemies?
- Why did his disciples have so little faith while a poor widow had so much?
- How many fish and bagels would it take to feed 5,000 men?
- Why did Jesus associate with outcasts?
- How did Jesus handle criticism? Or a hostile press conference?
- How did he deal with interruptions? What did his date book look like?
- Did he leave a will? Did he have anything to leave?
- How many people showed up to celebrate Jesus' resurrection at the first Easter sunrise service?
- Why did fickle Peter die for the same person he had earlier denied?

The life of Jesus is the central focus of the Bible, the number one best-seller of all time. Aside from the divinity of Jesus, how do you explain the origin of the Bible? How could forty different men living 1,600 years apart, most of whom never knew each other, speaking different languages, living in different countries, and having different cultures and careers, write a sixty-six-book cohesive work about a Mideastern rabbi? And even if they could write it, who would compile it? Or read it? Or believe it? Or die for it?

Recently when our family returned from a vacation, there were newspapers in plastic bags strewn all over our yard (I had forgotten to call the paper to stop delivery). I searched through them all to find the current paper and then threw the other yellowed ones away. Why? Because they were old news.

But the story of Jesus is not stale news. His Book is not like yesterday's newspaper. Nor does it need to be updated monthly like the books in our law library.

Jesus' story is timeless, changeless, endless—Jesus is online, yesterday, today, and forever. He is the Word perfect. Through him we have instant access to the Father twenty-four hours a day.

The purpose of this book is to make the life of Jesus relevant today—to tell the old, old story in a new way.

So let's go back in time and put ourselves into his stories. Let's sit with him on the Galilee docks as he dangles his feet in the water. Let's watch a leper with open sores make his way toward Jesus. Let's walk some dusty roads with him, with this incredible being who was both human and divine.

What would it have been like back then? Just imagine.

Part 1

# Little Jesus

## The Quiet Years

# 1

# In the Beginning

In the beginning, God created heaven and earth. And the earth was formless and empty and dark. So God turned on the light. That was Day 1. God liked what he saw and said it was good.

The next day, God began to fashion his creation. He contoured the earth with mountains and rolling hills. He spoke and—poof!—crystal clear waters flowed 'round the earth. God's self-analysis: So far, so good.

Day 3. It was time for some ground cover, so God laid down soil and rocks and trees—some fruit bearing, some for shade. The rest of the earth he covered with sand and a carpet of lush, green grass. God's interim grade: Good.

The next day he looked at the empty heavens. He crafted a sun to warm the trees, then hung a moon and ten zillion stars. All the lights came on. His self-grade? Good.

## God's Report Card

**Subject:** *Universe Creation*

| Date | | Created | Self-grade |
|------|---|---------|------------|
| Day | 1 | Heaven and earth | A |
| Day | 2 | Waters and land | A |
| Day | 3 | Grass and trees | A |
| Day | 4 | Sun and moon | A |
| Day | 5 | Animals and birds | A |
| Day | 6 | Adam and Eve | A+ |
| Day | 7 | Recess | |

On the fifth day newly formed earth was ready for life, so God created some animals—cows and cats on the grass, fish and sharks in the seas, birds and parrots in the skies. Listen to their sounds. Planet Earth had come alive. God's grade: Another good—straight As.

Then God decided to wrap things up, saying, "Let's make man in our own image." As he spoke, he scooped up some dust, and the first man appeared.

Minutes later God put first man to sleep and performed first surgery to produce first woman. First marriage was performed. And God said at the wedding, "Very good." Excellent. A+.

God told Adam, "Welcome to the garden. Take care of it. It's all yours. You are free to eat from any tree in the garden, except one. If you eat of the Tree of the Knowledge of Good and Evil, you will die."

The choice was Adam's—enjoy the garden and live, or partake of the forbidden tree and die.

And man chose death. A pall fell over the universe that God had created—over the animals and over mankind. All creation groaned. Sin marred perfect beauty. The die had been cast. Adam, get a job!

So how does an all-loving yet all-just God bridge the chasm between himself and his creation that has separated itself from him? When Plan A goes astray, does God have a Plan B to reunite God and man? How can God save his people from their sins?

That's where Jesus comes in.

In the words of Jill Briscoe, "When Eve ate the apple in the garden, Jesus began to pack his bags for Bethlehem."

# 2

# Wonderful Counselor

While we were vacationing in Bermuda several years ago, a bank down the street was robbed. The bank had opened early for employees, and the robber forced his way inside. He scooped up some money in a large sack, fired a shot into the ceiling, then jumped a fence behind the bank and sped away on a minibike. The total elapsed time: less than four minutes.

The police arrived at the bank moments later. The chief dispatched officers in boats to search the coast. He also set up a roadblock to search all vehicles leaving that end of the island.

Another officer gathered all the eyewitnesses in a conference room and asked them to describe the suspect in detail. Shortly afterward, a police artist arrived and began to sketch a composite picture of a man he had never seen, only heard about from various verbal descriptions.

Within an hour, the sketch was finished, and copies appeared on TV and in handbills. The sketch was so remarkably accurate that some residents immediately recognized the suspect and gave his location to the police. He was apprehended that afternoon, and the police artist was later credited for the quick arrest.

All of that was done to identify and ultimately capture a criminal. God used a similar technique to announce his son, not a criminal of course, but the Son of God. The prophets painted a composite picture of the coming Messiah hundreds of years before his arrival. Stroke by stroke and line upon line, they described this Promised One.

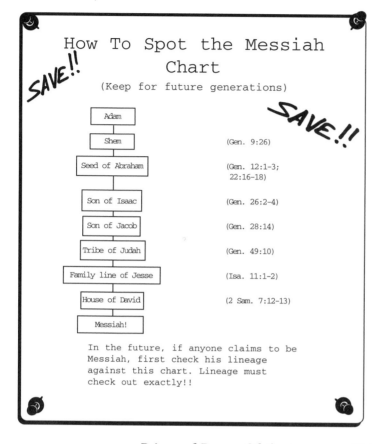

## How To Spot the Messiah Chart

SAVE!! SAVE!!

(Keep for future generations)

|  |  |
|---|---|
| Adam | |
| Shem | (Gen. 9:26) |
| Seed of Abraham | (Gen. 12:1-3; 22:16-18) |
| Son of Isaac | (Gen. 26:2-4) |
| Son of Jacob | (Gen. 28:14) |
| Tribe of Judah | (Gen. 49:10) |
| Family line of Jesse | (Isa. 11:1-2) |
| House of David | (2 Sam. 7:12-13) |
| Messiah! | |

In the future, if anyone claims to be Messiah, first check his lineage against this chart. Lineage must check out exactly!!

From the prophets' collective clues, the people could visualize a man they had never seen. They would recognize Messiah when he arrived.

*Clue 1—His mother.* The prophet Isaiah gave us the most unusual clue—the Messiah would be born of a virgin. "The Lord himself will choose the sign—the child shall be born to a virgin! And she shall call him Immanuel (meaning, 'God with us')" (Isa. 7:14).

*Clue 2—His name.* Isaiah also described some of Messiah's qualities and titles: "For unto us a child is born, unto us a son is given: and the government shall be upon his shoulder: and his name shall be called Wonderful, Counsellor, The mighty God, The everlasting Father, The Prince of Peace. Of the increase of his government and peace there will be no end" (Isa. 9:6–7 KJV).

*Clue 3—His birthplace.* Where would the King of Kings be born? A major city like Jerusalem or perhaps Rome? How about Cairo? No. It would be the tiny village of Bethlehem, predicted by the prophet Micah. "O Bethlehem Ephrathah, you are but a small Judean village, yet you will be the birthplace of my King who is alive from everlasting ages past!" (Micah 5:2).

Hundreds of years later, when Joseph arrived in Bethlehem, he was right on the divine schedule. He pulled into the City of David, the predetermined birthplace, just as Mary prepared to deliver her precious heavenly cargo—the Son of God.

Other prophecies were given hundreds of years before Jesus, causing historians and theologians to keep track of these references. Even King Herod quizzed the wise men concerning where Scripture prophesied Messiah would be born. The world was awaiting his arrival, confident they would recognize him from his advance descriptions.

# 3

# Good News Babies

"Messiah is coming! Messiah is coming!" announced the prophets Micah and Isaiah to the nation of Israel, a people starved for good news.

But when? Next year? Two years? Ten years? For forty years the children of Israel wandered in the desert, hoping, "Surely, Messiah will come soon."

But no. Fifty years passed. Then 100 more years, leaving great-grandchildren to wonder, "Has God forgotten his promise? Did we miss the Messiah?"

And suddenly, 400 years after the prophets' proclamation, a divine messenger appeared—not dressed as a UPS delivery man but as an angel. A sparkling, dazzling, super-being appeared to Zechariah, an elderly priest, in the temple.

Six months later, the same angel returned for another announcement—this time to Mary, a newly engaged teenager, to say that the young virgin would miraculously give birth to the Messiah.

Let's compare their announcements and reactions in Luke 1. The angelic announcements to each (1) gave words of personal comfort to the listener, (2) then described the babies to be born, and (3) finally closed with a question and answer period.

# ANNOUNCEMENTS BY ANGEL GABRIEL

### 1. Personal words to Zechariah and Mary

| To Zechariah, father-to-be of John the Baptist (Luke 1:13) | To Mary, mother-to-be of Jesus (Luke 1:30–31) |
|---|---|
| "Don't be afraid."<br>"God has heard your prayer."<br>"Your wife Elizabeth will bear you a son."<br><br>"You are to name him John." | "Don't be frightened."<br>"God has decided to wonderfully bless you!"<br>"Very soon now, you will become pregnant and have a baby boy."<br>"You are to name him 'Jesus.'" |

### 2. Qualities of each son-to-be

| John the Baptist (Luke 1:15–17) | Jesus (Luke 1:32–33) |
|---|---|
| "Will be one of the Lord's great men."<br>"Will be filled with the Holy Spirit, even from before his birth!"<br>"Will persuade many a Jew to turn to the Lord his God."<br>"Will precede the coming of the Messiah, preparing the people for his arrival." | "Shall be very great."<br>"Shall be called the Son of God."<br>"Lord God will give him the throne of his ancestor David."<br>"Shall reign over Israel forever."<br>"His kingdom shall never end." |

### 3. Questions to angel

| By Zechariah (Luke 1:18) | By Mary (Luke 1:34) |
|---|---|
| Q: "But this is impossible! I'm an old man now, and my wife is also well along in years." | Q: "How can I have a baby? I am a virgin." |

### 4. Angel's response

| To Zechariah (Luke 1:20) | To Mary (Luke 1:35, 37) |
|---|---|
| "Because you haven't believed me, you are to be stricken silent, unable to speak until the child is born."<br><br>"For my words will certainly come true at the proper time." | "The Holy Spirit shall come upon you and the power of God shall overshadow you; so the baby born to you will be utterly holy—the Son of God."<br>"For every promise from God shall surely come true." |

# 4

# When Angels Speak

As I read about angelic appearances, it's easy to think that these supernatural announcements were taken in stride by an elderly priest and a teenage virgin. After all, this was during Bible times, and as the characters selected to play each part, they were expecting announcements like this every day. Right?

Wrong!

Would it have been any different if an angel appeared to someone today? Imagine if an angel had appeared in a mall parking lot to Peter Larson, a retired butcher in Cleveland. Wouldn't his reaction have been as incredulous? Do butchers from Cleveland expect angel visits in parking lots?

And then what about Larson's friends? Imagine the conversation the next day when Mr. Larson tells his barber, "Hey, Bill, you'd never guess what happened to me last night!"

"Lemme guess. You and the missus went to the Senior Citizens Dance?"

"Nope."

"Won the condo shuffleboard tournament?"

"Nope. You'll never guess. Saw an angel! Bright shining, even spoke to me!"

"Sure you did. What'd she look like?"

"No, I'm serious . . ."

# UFO

## SIGHTINGS

### J o u r n a l

Jerusalem  • BULLETIN TO ALL SUBSCRIBERS •  Edition

## Two "Angel" Sightings Reported

In recent weeks, two similar UFO sightings have been reported—one in Jerusalem and the other in Nazareth, the small town fifteen miles southwest of Galilee.

An elderly temple priest named Zechariah (who is not a subscriber) reported the first rather unusual sighting. He wrote, "I saw a brilliant 'angel' who spoke to me (in Hebrew, no less) and almost blinded me, it was so bright."

The priest reported that when he questioned this "angel," he couldn't speak from then on. He answered our interview questions on a blackboard. But though he lost his voice, he didn't lose his humor; he wrote, "The angel left me speechless!"

What was the message he heard from the alleged angel? Zechariah and his elderly wife will have a baby! Most unlikely, considering their ages. A couple of fertile octogenarians!

The other sighting was reported six months later by Mary, sixteen, a teenager from Nazareth, who also claims she saw a brilliant Hebrew-speaking being. The message given to her was even more bizarre: She'll have a baby, but get this—she's a virgin!

While these "beings of light" seem to conform to the patterns of other sightings, their messages have been unusual, to say the least. Zechariah's speech loss may be the result of an alien-inflicted injury or a traumatic response to the sighting. If this were a visitation by alien beings, it is totally different from any we've seen before. And the skeptics among us still think it's just a convenient story to cover a youthful indiscretion.

One other note: The two "mothers-to-be" in these reports—Mary and Elizabeth—are cousins, which makes the whole business even more questionable. We don't know what kind of scam they're cooking up, but we urge our readers to disregard these stories. However, the *Journal* will be keeping tabs on this story—just in case. If any supernatural things begin to happen, we'll let you know.

"Peter, please keep your voice down. Have you been feeling all right lately? Too much sun maybe?"

And then can't you imagine the conversation an hour later when Mr. Larson leaves the barbershop? "Jack, never guess what happened to old Peter Larson last night."

"His dentures slid down the drain?"

"Nope, crazier than that. He saw one of them . . . well, how do you say it? One of them strange sightings things. Actually spoke to him, too."

"Think he's got a screw loose?"

"Could be, although he seemed sincere!"

"That's the way it starts. Poor Peter! And hey, Bill, don't take too much off the top. I need all I got left."

I believe that angel sightings in Israel years ago were as unlikely as they are today, and I imagine that the level of skepticism was every bit the same.

Maybe the local press would have covered these angelic appearances in the *UFO Sightings Journal* (see page 24).

### How to Respond to an Angel

Most etiquette books have a special chapter on how to address royalty, but I haven't seen any books on how to respond to an angel, aka "Angel Protocol." Fortunately, in Luke's Gospel, we have at least two different accounts of actual angel arrivals—one from a teenager and the other from a senior citizen. Zechariah doubted the angel's message at first and was unable to speak until after his baby boy was born. Mary was also amazed at the angel's message, but she believed it to be true.

In response to these miraculous events, Zechariah and Mary gave separate, yet symmetrically parallel verses of praise to God, inspired by the Holy Spirit. Their hearts literally overflowed with joy as they anticipated the coming of the Holy Child and his forerunner.

Note especially the lack of any references to self. Zechariah and Mary focused all their attention on Messiah to come. No personal requests, only praise to him.

These passages are so grand in style and content that a local Judean publisher might have tried to promote an inspirational poster capitalizing on these words of praise.

---

# pPp

Petra Poster Publishers

To: Herman, Sales Manager
From: Nathan, Marketing Director
Re: Angel Speak Poster

Next month, we will be adding a new poster to our Motivational and Inspirational Poster Line. Not another sales training poster, this one contains quotes from a priest and a teenager immediately after each one was told they would be having children under most unusual circumstances.

There are remarkable similarities between these two works, even though they were written by an elderly male and a young female about seventy years apart in age, apparently without collaboration.

Esther, our Fine Literature assistant, after reviewing these writings and interviewing the writers, said, "It's amazing that these were written by people without any literary background." Wilcox, our Department Chairman, wrote me, "These writings are ethereal and unique in that they are totally non-self-centered. It is almost as though some divine spirit inspired each writing because the style is so similar and praise producing."

If the posters sell well, we may consider setting these lyrics to music and selling praise T-shirts.

The posters should have widespread appeal across generational lines. We've got both the teenage and the senior citizen markets covered, and if Messiah should come, we'll be the first to cash in!

Good luck!

# Celebration of Life

**Zechariah, 89**
**"Benedictus" (Luke 1:68–79)**

"Praise the Lord, the God of Israel, for he has come to visit his people and has redeemed them.

"He is sending us a Mighty Savior from the royal line of his servant David, just as he promised through his holy prophets long ago—someone to save us from our enemies, from all who hate us.

"He has been merciful to our ancestors, yes, to Abraham himself, by remembering his sacred promise to him, and by granting us the privilege of serving God fearlessly, freed from our enemies, and by making us holy and acceptable, ready to stand in his presence forever.

"And you, my little son, shall be called the prophet of the glorious God, for you will prepare the way for the Messiah. You will tell his people how to find salvation through forgiveness of their sins.

"All this will be because the mercy of our God is very tender, and heaven's dawn is about to break upon us, to give light to those who sit in darkness and death's shadow, and to guide us to the path of peace."

**Mary, 16**
**"Magnificat" (Luke 1:46–55)**

"Oh, how I praise the Lord. How I rejoice in God my Savior!

"For he took notice of his lowly servant girl, and now generation after generation forever shall call me blest of God.

"For he, the mighty Holy One, has done great things to me.

"His mercy goes on from generation to generation, to all who reverence him.

"How powerful is his mighty arm!

"How he scatters the proud and haughty ones!

"He has torn princes from their thrones and exalted the lowly.

"He has satisfied the hungry hearts and sent the rich away with empty hands.

"And how he has helped his servant Israel!

"He has not forgotten his promise to be merciful.

"For he promised our fathers—Abraham and his children—to be merciful to them forever."

The same angel was sent as a courier from heaven to deliver two historic birth announcements. Although these private announcements were given secretly to the parents, they would be made known to the world at the appointed time. "The Messiah is coming" meant good news to a troubled world.

# 5

# Dr. Luke's Dinner Party

```
You are cordially invited

for dinner

at

Dr. and Mrs. Luke's house

when

next Thursday evening

time

1:00 P.M.

purpose

Just to unwind with a few close friends.
A unique slide show will follow dinner.
We hope you can come. Dress casual.

RSVP 386
```

What was life like for Luke, a Mideastern doctor who lived during the time of Jesus? As a physician, Dr. Luke's schedule was not his own. As he cared for the needs of his townspeople, from the homeless to the mayor, he was undoubtedly on call twenty-four hours a day.

Luke also moonlighted as a historian. He probably took sabbaticals from time to time to travel and conduct research.

I can imagine Dr. Luke returning from a research trip to Galilee, his duffle bag packed with pictures and notes from interviews with Zechariah and Elizabeth and Mary. Let's grab a pita while we catch his slide show with a few close friends.

\*     \*     \*

Good evening, friends. Miriam and I are delighted that all of you could join us for dinner this evening. We have a few slides that we thought you'd enjoy. No Jim, none of the kids, I promise. Or me floating in the Dead Sea, or Miriam on the camel.

I have assembled these slides from a number of sources. I haven't shown them before, so this is a first and very private showing.

Miriam, if you'd blow out the lamp, we can begin.

You may have heard of this fellow—Zechariah the priest. He's right there in the synagogue praying for Messiah to come, just as he's prayed for over fifty years. He's eighty-nine.

*Click.* This slide is overexposed, but it's kept in sequence because it's significant. That's Zechariah to the left, and the bright light is an angel. I'm serious! This is a *brilliant* angel. In fact, I think it's the first angel ever photographed. The *Jerusalem Enquirer* offered a thousand drachmas for this shot alone. The angel is saying, "Zechariah, you're going to be a daddy!"

*Click.* Here's Zack laughing.

*Click.* Here's Zack writing a note to Elizabeth on his slate. For those of you who forgot your glasses, the fine print reads, "I can't speak, but an angel told me we're going to have a baby."

*Click.* Here's Elizabeth laughing and telling Zack, "Me, have a baby at ninety-two? That's a good one! Talk to me Zack! Put down that slate!"

*Click.* Here's another note back from Zack, "Liz, I'm serious! And I can't talk."

*Click.* And here's Elizabeth again, "What's with this slate action, Zack? Are you playing charades?"

*Click.* Here's Zack underlining the words, "I'm serious!"

*Click.* Now we're back to Elizabeth, who just said, "Zack, I can't take this flying leap. Here I'm drawing Medicare, and you're talking baby showers. We're going from the nursing home to the nursery? From dentures to diapers? From a cane to a cradle?! Can't you just see us at PTA meetings?!"

*Click.* Now here we are several months later in Nazareth, in a lower-class neighborhood. The pretty brunette doing dishes is Mary, cleaning up after breakfast. Her father just left for work, and her mother's at the grocery. That's their new coffeepot she's drying.

*Click.* This next picture was taken seconds later. Again, excuse the overexposure, but the photographer never anticipated another angel sighting—especially at the kitchen sink! The angel just told Mary she'll be Messiah's mother. "Me?" Mary's stunned. That's her coffeepot in pieces on the floor.

By the way, speaking of coffee, if any of you would like some, Miriam still has half a pot left. Or you can catch it later when we light the lamps. We're almost finished, Ben. Now back to the slides.

*Click.* See Mary run. She's running to meet her great-aunt, Elizabeth.

*Click.* Here's Mary out of breath at the front door. Elizabeth is six months pregnant. At ninety-two? Wrinkled face and pregnant body? Mary says, "Aunt Elizabeth, no way!" "Way!" Elizabeth responds.

*Click.* Meanwhile back at Nazareth, here's Mary's fiancé, a worried young man named Joseph, pacing the floor and thinking, "Where's Mary? Why did she take off so fast? It's not like her to break our date. Did I say something? Is there someone else?"

*Click.* Three months later. Mary has returned to Nazareth. Here she is with Joseph in a park, but why is she crying?

*Click.* Check out the expression on Joseph's face. Mary's pregnant, but it's not his child. Wow, is he mad! And confused!

*Click.* Here's another overexposure. Angel sighting number three—to Joseph this time, later that night. "It's OK," says the angel. "The father is the Holy Spirit." Joseph realizes the miracle and believes. His suspicion melts away. His face spells relief.

*Click.* The wedding is back on. Here's Mary addressing wedding invitations. That's a *Bride* magazine on her desk.

*Click.* Here are Joseph and Mary in a long line at the Nazareth post office. They're waiting to pick up their letters from Governor Cyrenius requiring each family to register.

*Click.* Their letters say to report to Bethlehem.

*Click.* Joseph and his about-to-deliver wife are leaving Nazareth. Ever ride a mile on a donkey? Try a hundred! And try it pregnant! It's brutal! Or so I'm told.

*Click.* Here's a sign at the Jerusalem Hilton—"No Vacancy."

*Click.* Here's the Mount of Olives Sheraton—"No Vacancy."

*Click.* Here's the Bethlehem Holiday Inn—"No Vacancy."

*Click.* Here's Joseph back at the front desk, pleading with the reservations clerk, pointing to his wife outside, who is doubled over.

*Click.* Here's the hotel manager shaking his head. "Sorry!"

*Click.* Now this picture is underexposed, very hard to see. Sorry about that. We're inside a barn behind the motel. You can barely see the dark stable. That's Mary lying in the straw behind those cows. All alone and in pain. She's scared.

*Click.* This is about an hour later. Now Mary's face is radiant. She's beaming, holding her tiny baby wrapped in rags. Laughing and crying tears of joy!

*Click.* That's Joseph behind Mary, grinning from ear to ear, with his arms around her.

*Click.* Here's a close-up of the baby—Baby Messiah, asleep on the hay.

*Click.* Now here's another overexposure. Didn't anticipate another angel sighting. This time thousands of them. Singing. Performing a private concert celebrating the birth of Baby Jesus. Merry Christmas, Planet Earth!

# 6

# Home Alone Thirty

Have you ever wondered why we don't know more about Jesus as a child? as a teenager? or as a young man? There were three decades of near silence while Jesus was preparing for his last three years on earth. Thirty years of private preparation for three of public ministry. A ten to one ratio for Jesus Christ.

What was Jesus' home like? Where did the Son of God go to school, or did he? Was he on the honor roll? Who were his friends? Where did he work? Did he date? Did he catch the flu? Was he the life of the party? Did he perform miracles? Did he play sports?

Why did Jesus wait until age thirty to begin his public ministry? Nowhere does Scripture indicate that Jesus performed a single miracle before age thirty. Not one. Not even a healing. Except for one brief moment when he dazzled rabbis in the temple at age twelve, Jesus didn't seem to make much of a splash. In his neighborhood, he was just a carpenter.

Just a carpenter, who was also a very nice guy.

Just a carpenter, who never cheated customers.

Just a carpenter, whose furniture was exceptional.

Nonetheless, just a carpenter. Nothing more.

How about Jesus' cousin, John the Baptist? How did John keep his own special mission secret for thirty long years? Did John know that Jesus was the Messiah? As teenagers at play, do you think John and Jesus talked about John's role as divine messenger?

And how about Jesus' mother, Mary, who had been given a special secret years before? All those intimate yet powerful birth promises that Jesus would save his people from their sins. Mary must have wondered, "When will it happen?" How was Mary able to keep quiet during her teenage years until she was almost fifty? When friends stopped by to tell praise stories about Jesus, how she must have been tempted to say, "You haven't seen anything yet!" Yet the Scriptures report she "treasured all these things in her heart" (Luke 2:51 NIV).

And Mary had lots to keep inside and to treasure:

- She received royal visitors to a dirty stable bringing gold and perfume to the newborn babe.
- She fled across a scorching Arabian desert to save her baby from Herod's death squads.
- Her model preteen got left behind on a family trip because he was confounding scribes with his brilliance.

Lots of questions were left unanswered during Jesus' early years. Yet we know that while he was 100 percent man, he was tempted like a man, but as 100 percent God, he was without sin. Other than that, we know very little about his first thirty years of life, and what we do know would probably fit into his mother's small scrapbook.

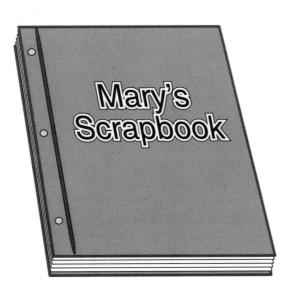

**P. Sulpicius Quirinius**

*Governor, Syria*

CERTIFIED MAIL

In the XXIV year
of Caesar Augustus

Joseph, Carpenter
18 Main Street
Nazareth

Please be advised that pursuant to an Executive Order of His
Excellency, the Emperor Augustus Caesar, the Roman
Government will be taking a worldwide census next month. Each
resident is required to travel to the town that was formerly the
registered town of the family.

According to the last census records, your ancestral home is
Bethlehem, in Judea.

Therefore, within thirty days from receipt of this letter, you are
required to report to Bethlehem, the City of David, to register.
There are no exceptions.

PLEASE GOVERN YOURSELF ACCORDINGLY.

*P. SULPICIUS QUIRINIUS*

Governor, Syria

# Certificate of Live Birth

### Judea

Bethlehem Board of Health
Bureau of Vital Statistics

Birth No. 3487
Registrar's No. 421

1. Child's Name: *Jesus*
2. Date of Birth: *23rd day, Kislev, 3755*
3. Sex: *Male*
4. Race: *Jewish*
5. Birthplace: *Bethlehem, Judea*
6. Hospital Name: *None (stable behind inn)*
7. Mother's Name: *Mary*
8. Residence: *18 Main Street, Nazareth*
9. Father's Name: *Joseph*

*I certify that the above named child was born alive at the place and time and on the date stated above.*

10. Signature: _Joseph_  _Mary_

Father     Mother

---

# Certificate of Circumcision

Be it known that

# Jesus

having fulfilled the requirements of this Temple,
is hereby
dedicated as circumcised in this State.

In witness whereof, I have hereunto set my hand and
affixed the seal of the Supreme Temple, at Jerusalem,
this 31st day of Kislev, 3755

_Nicodemus_

*High Priest, Jerusalem Temple*

## Visitors Log—Bethlehem

| Name | Address | Baby Gifts | Thank Yous Written |
|------|---------|------------|--------------------|
| 1. Shepherds | Bethlehem | Lamb | X |
| 2. Angels | Heaven | Music | X (verbal) |
| 3. Magi | Far East | Gold, oils, perfumes myrrh | X |

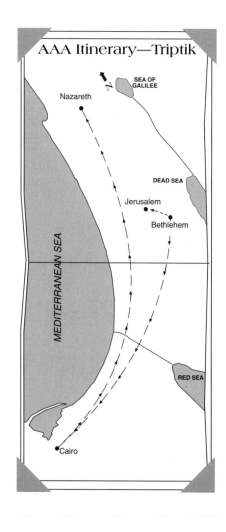

AAA Itinerary—Triptik

SEA OF GALILEE

Nazareth

DEAD SEA

Jerusalem

Bethlehem

MEDITERRANEAN SEA

RED SEA

Cairo

The Nazareth Synagogue
has conferred on

# Jesus

this Certificate of
Bar Mitzvah
and all the rights and privileges thereunto appertaining.
In Witness Whereof, this Certificate, duly signed,
has been issued and the seal of the Synagogue affixed,
this 23rd day of Kislev, 3768

High Priest (seal)

*Nicodemus*
Pharisee

Jesus' First Hammer age 9

## Carpenters Union
### Application

Name:

*Jesus*

Age:

*12 years old*

Address:

*18 Main Street, Nazareth*

Experience:

*none*

---

## Jerusalem Gazette

## Kid Amazes Rabbis

JERUSALEM—A twelve-year-old boy from Nazareth named Jesus suddenly appeared at the Temple Saturday to ask difficult questions of the rabbis on hand. For hours, the young Jesus pumped the rabbis, who then sought answers from the youngster. "Where did he come from?" asked one observer. Aaron knew the child's parents, Mary and Joseph, but said, "The kid's vast knowledge is amazing without formal schooling."

---

### Interim Grade

During Jesus' first thirty years of life on earth, God Almighty was physically present here. Yet that's all we know about those years. Thirty quiet years. Years of preparation. We *do* know that Jesus grew in favor with men and, more important, with God (Luke 2:52).

When he reached age thirty, the first chapter of Jesus' life as a young man was about to close, and a new one, the reason for which he came, was about to begin.

What would Jesus' report card have looked like for the first thirty years, graded by Instructor God the Father?

---

### The Report Card of
*Jesus Christ*

Grade

Favor with man   *A+*
Favor with God   *A+*

This is my beloved Son, and I am wonderfully pleased with him.

(signed) __**God Almighty**__

---

# Part 2

# Thirtysomething
## 1,000 Days—
## "We Hardly Knew You"

# 7

# First-Time Events

In 1991, Major League Baseball awarded a new franchise to the Florida Marlins. For the next two years, Miami residents eagerly anticipated what the Marlins team would be like. The excitement level rose as players and coaches were selected.

My wife, Marabel, and I were in the crowd for the inaugural game, along with 44,000 other wildly enthusiastic fanatics, most watching a big league game for the first time. This was one game that I'll never forget because each moment marked a first.

The Florida Marlins kept a careful list of their first-time events; not only the easy ones like the first strikeout, the first double play, and the first error, but also a few others[1]:

First ceremonial pitch—Joe DiMaggio
First boo—introduction of the New York Mets flag
First foul ball caught by a fan—Michael Cornley
First beach ball in stands—2:09 P.M., first base line
First bat to go flying—Orel Hershiser in the third inning

But the first-time events of a baseball team can't hold a candle to the first-time events when Jesus Christ stepped into the spotlight. He had been in spring training (in a league of his own), and now his time had come. Here are some of his special first-time events when he announced to the public who he was—his thirty-year World's Best-Kept Secret.

### First Announcement by Advance Man

The first announcement of Jesus' arrival was made by John the Baptist, Jesus' cousin. Who was this cave-dwelling, wilderness-walking, animal-skin-dressing, locusts-and-honey-eating, fire and brimstone preacher? None other than John—the advance man for the still-sidelined Jesus.

John stepped forward to make the joyous announcement the world had awaited for 1,500 years: "The kingdom of heaven is at hand. . . . Prepare ye the way of the Lord" (Matt. 3:2–3 KJV). "I baptize you with water. . . . But after me will come one who is more powerful than I, whose sandals I am not fit to carry" (Matt. 3:11 NIV).

John the Baptist was commissioned to baptize the Messiah, at first against John's own wishes (*"I* baptize *you?!"*), but then as a willing servant.

As Jesus emerged from the water, the Holy Spirit in the form of a heavenly dove rested upon him. Enter Jesus, exit John. John's brief but important role was finished; Jesus would now take over. In the parting words of John, "He must become greater; I must become less" (John 3:30 NIV).

**First Temptation of Christ**

After Jesus was baptized, the Holy Spirit then led him from the sea to the sand, from the water to the wilderness, the same wilderness that John the Baptist had been calling his home. Yet at this time, Jesus was not called to preach but to pray. All alone he prayed—no disciples, no family, and no food. For more than a month, he fasted. And while Jesus was in this vulnerable, weakened physical condition, Satan himself tempted him continuously for forty days—(1) to turn stones into hot baked bread, (2) to worship Satan, and (3) to jump off a cliff without a bungee cord so angels could rescue him before he crashed. But these temptations were to no avail as Jesus repelled each one with powerful memorized Scripture verses.

- "Man does not live on bread alone" (Luke 4:4 NIV).
- "Worship the Lord your God and serve him only" (Luke 4:8 NIV).
- "Do not put the Lord your God to a foolish test" (Luke 4:12).

The first temptation of Christ was over. But more would come.

### First Divine Announcement by Jesus

Travel back to the dusty village of Nazareth, the hometown of Jesus, the virile, ever-friendly, and ever-considerate young carpenter. When the moment finally came for Jesus to reveal his true identity, how would he do it? Who would he tell? Maybe a few friends over dinner? Or maybe let his rabbi announce it? Perhaps write a book? Or call a press conference?

Jesus chose to preach a sermon. He selected his hometown synagogue—probably the same one that had given him perfect attendance medals years before.

The time of the announcement? A Sabbath morning when he usually read Hebrew Scriptures to his gathered family and neighbors all seated in their regular pews. But on this Sabbath morning, he didn't stand before them as Carpenter Jesus. This morning he stood as Messiah Jesus, Son of God.

It was no coincidence that the scroll handed to him that morning was from the prophet Isaiah, and Jesus began to read: "The Spirit of the Lord God is upon me, because the Lord has anointed me to bring good news to the suffering and afflicted. He has sent me to comfort the brokenhearted, to announce liberty to captives and to open the eyes of the blind. He has sent me to tell those who mourn that the time of God's favor to them has come" (Isa. 61:1–2).

It was no coincidence that following the Scripture reading, Jesus made the first announcement concerning his own divinity: "These Scriptures came true today!" (Luke 4:21).

Today. Not next week or next month. It starts now. Ladies and gentlemen, friends and neighbors, prophecy is fulfilled right before your very eyes. Jesus is the Lord's Anointed One, for whom Israel has been waiting these many centuries. He's the one, ten feet away.

Can't you imagine the reaction of the congregation?

"Excuse me, Martha, is your hearing aid on?"

"Isn't that the carpenter who built our table?"

"Nathan, did you catch what he said?"

Can't you imagine the reaction of the frustrated rabbi who stood up to preach his prepared sermon just as Jesus was sitting down? Regaining control of the service would be impossible. "Would you please be seated. Please take your seats. Please! The service isn't over . . . Well, I guess it is."

And can't you imagine the heart of Mary exploding with joy? Jesus' words had just confirmed the angel's words spoken to her thirty long years before. "It's true!" She was now free to tell the world her private personal experience. Joseph was *not* his father. Jesus was both God and man.

The prophets had declared, "The Messiah's coming"; the angel said, "He's almost here"; John the Baptist preached, "Get ready, he's right behind me"; and then Jesus said, "Here I am!"

### First Move by Jesus

By the time he was thirty, Jesus had already moved several times. The first move (excluding the heaven-to-Bethlehem trip) was from Bethlehem to Egypt (for at least two years), then it was on to Nazareth to live, with regular visits to Jerusalem for holy days.

But the first recorded move after Jesus announced his holy calling was from Nazareth to Capernaum. Nazareth was located in the mountains halfway between Galilee

```
┌─────────────────────────────────────────────┐
│                                             │
│  Change of Address Card                     │
│                                             │
│  Name:  Jesus                               │
│  Previous Address: 18 Main Street, Nazareth │
│                                             │
│  Business Name: Seashore Carpenter Shop     │
│  Street Address: 127 Lake Drive             │
│  City/Zip: Capernaum 321                    │
│                                             │
└─────────────────────────────────────────────┘
```

and the Mediterranean, near the well-traveled north-south highway running through Israel. Nazareth was a natural turnpike plaza for the multinational caravans that traveled this road. As he was growing up, Jesus may have helped international travelers as they sought directions and stocked up on supplies.

When Jesus moved from Nazareth to Capernaum, he went from hill country to seashore. Capernaum was the chief commercial center in Galilee. Business was brisk, and restaurants and shops were filled with Roman soldiers on leave from the large military base in town. This busy seacoast town would become Jesus' first mission field.

How did Jesus tell his family he would be leaving for Capernaum? Perhaps he told them one night after dinner. The next morning when he awoke early, I can imagine him packing his meager possessions, then kissing his family good-bye. It had to be a tearful farewell for Mary (Joseph may have been dead by then) and his brothers and sisters.

I can see them watching while Jesus headed north on the highway, waving to them with one hand, carrying a bag in the other. Undoubtedly he had no advance hotel reservations.

I suppose his twenty-five-mile trip to Capernaum would take him a day or two. He was in strong physical shape.

He would walk alone.

### First Sermon of Jesus

Jesus was a man of few words. His first divine announcement took only five words: "These Scriptures came true today!" His first recorded sermon in the Capernaum synagogue was only eight words long: "Repent, for the kingdom of heaven is near."

This was the same sermon that John the Baptist had preached before Jesus picked up the theme. When John preached in a hot desert, he drew huge crowds. When Jesus preached the same sermon in Capernaum, he too attracted multitudes.

"Repent, for the kingdom of heaven is near." That's all the Scripture records for Jesus' first sermon. Eight words short in length, but strong in impact. Was that all he said in this sermon? Maybe not, but the message was clear.

As Jesus continued preaching, the crowds grew larger, the meetings became more frequent, yet the message remained the same.

I imagine that after each sermon, discussions in coffee shops centered not so much on what was said but rather

> **Capernaum Synagogue**
> Service
> 6:00 P.M.
> Speaker: Jesus
> Sermon Title:
> **Repent**

on what was meant. What was this "kingdom of heaven," and how was it near? Would Israel overthrow Roman rule? Will there be peace on earth? One world government? Who will be in charge, and more important, how does one get in on the control group?

### First Disciple Called by Jesus

Andrew was an energetic young fisherman, a man on the move. He was a most unlikely candidate for a sudden career change. But when he met the Master, all that changed. Andrew was the first disciple called by Jesus. He told his brother Simon Peter, "We have found the Messiah!" (John 1:41).

Visit Lovely Galilee

Peter,
  Wish you were here!

          Andrew

### First Recorded Miracle of Jesus

The first miracle that Jesus performed was at a wedding reception when the wine had run out. Jesus was present as an invited guest (he never goes where he's not invited), and he recognized the problem. Would the Master use this night of celebration to demonstrate his divine power for the first time?

You bet! First, he asked the waiters to fill six stone pots with water, about twenty to thirty gallons each. "Fill them to the brim," he said.

Then he said, "Dip some out and take it to the master of ceremonies."

Once the host tasted it he knew that this was the best wine he'd ever tasted. The party continued on into the night! (John 2:1–11).

*Thank You!!*

Dear Jesus,
  We don't know exactly what you did at our wedding reception, but the wine steward sure was happy. Thanks so much. Having a great honeymoon in Crete. See you soon!

          Jason and Naomi

### First Show of Force by Jesus

When Jews came to worship at the temple in Jerusalem, they were required to sacrifice a bird or animal without blemish.

## MEMO

From: Chief, Temple Security
To:     All Temple money changers
Re:     Jesus' rampage last Friday

So sorry about what happened when Jesus drove you out of the Temple on Friday. If he ever does that again, we will prosecute to the fullest extent of the law.

At the temple, money changers provided a convenient one-stop shopping service that was especially appreciated by out-of-town worshipers who could purchase animals for sacrifice and exchange their foreign currency.

Jesus entered the temple and accused the money changers of converting it into a "den of thieves." His Holy Place was not to be Central Commerce, nor was the sacred to be secular. So Jesus the Peacemaker became Jesus the Whipmaker. He chased out the money changers and their animals. He overturned their tables, scattering money all over the floor, and exhorted them, "Don't turn my Father's house into a market" (John 2:14–16).

Draft
To: Ira Clayborne, Senior Editor
From: Ezra Haggaion, Cub Reporter

*Mr. Clayborne:*
*You wanted a sidebar to the money changer story. How's this?*
*EH*

*EH*
*Too Cute*

## GALILEAN THREATENS TO RAZE AND RAISE TEMPLE

JERUSALEM . . . After storming the temple courts and upsetting the tables of the money changers, Jesus of Nazareth hinted that he had bigger plans for the future. *vague!*
"Destroy this temple," said the itinerant preacher, "and I will rebuild it in three days."
Abel ben-Tabnit, chief contractor on the temple reconstruction, noted that the current building project had taken forty-six years already. "I don't know how he plans to do that," commented ben-Tabnit. "The Romans are working on some sort of hydraulics, but a structure like this would still take years, even without unionized labor."
A source close to the high priest indicated that this ridiculous comment is just another evidence of the carpenter-cum-preacher's lunacy.

*This is absolute lunacy! Did he really say this?! Vic.*

### First Recorded Reference to Jesus' Own Death

The Pharisees confronted Jesus after he had overthrown the money changers and challenged his authority. "Who are you to even dare to speak in *our* temple?"

"If you have this authority from God, show us a miracle to prove it," they challenged him.

Jesus replied, "This is the miracle I will do for you: Destroy this sanctuary and in three days I will raise it up!" (John 2:19). He was referring, of course, to his own body.

### First Private Interview of Jesus by a Religious Leader

One night, a Pharisee named Nicodemus came to meet Jesus (John 3:1–2). Why he came at night isn't mentioned nor how and who scheduled the appointment. Nicodemus was probably too busy to get away during the day, or perhaps he couldn't fight the huge crowds around Jesus, or perhaps he was afraid of being seen with Jesus. Whatever the case, he met Jesus at night—the first known Pharisee to come forward from an otherwise hostile group of religious leaders.

The interviewer (Nicodemus) asked how one could enter this kingdom of God, and the interviewee (Jesus) told about being born again—not physically but spiritually.

**7 WJER** A stuffy religious leader meets an offbeat rabbi and gets a new lease on life. Starring Nicodemus and Jesus.

---

[1]Special thanks to H. Wayne Huizenga, owner of the Florida Marlins, for providing the list of firsts concerning the team.

# 8

# Impossible Dreams

Jesus' first recorded miracle, according to John, was turning water into wine at a wedding reception. John gave us a detailed narrative of the occasion, including the problem (no wine), the miracle (150 gallons of water turned into fine wine), and even actual quotes of the guests ("They saved the best stuff for the last!").

This was only the first of many other miracles of Jesus. There would be more—lots more, tons more. How many, we'll never know. Several times Scripture says that Jesus healed "all those who came to him." That number could have been dozens or hundreds or even thousands.

In fact John reported that Jesus did "many other miracles besides the ones told about in this book." He also wrote that the world could not hold the books of all that Jesus did.

I am a detail person. I love to keep lists. I even keep lists of lists! Had I been an original disciple, I would have been the historian. I would have loved the challenge of keeping a detailed log of his miracles. If I had seen Jesus turn water to wine, the next time around I would have started my list something like the one on the next page.

So why did all four gospel reporters combined (Matthew, Mark, Luke, and John) only report thirty-five miracles of Jesus? Only thirty-five. Think about it. That's only about one a month for the three years of his public ministry. And John, the same one who told about the miracles en masse, only covered seven. Why?

John described the seven miracles "so that you will believe that he is the Messiah, the Son of God, and that believing in him you will

# Log—Jesus' Miracles
## by Disciple Charlie

| Date | Time | Place | Problem | Miracle |
|------|------|-------|---------|---------|
| 4/13/30 | 9:34 P.M. | Jason's wedding | No more wine | Turned 150 gallons of water to wine |
| 4/15/30 | 8:45 A.M. | Galilee beach | Official's son, sick | Healed |
| | 8:58 A.M. | Galilee beach | Boy, 9, blue shirt, crippled | Healed |
| | 9:13 A.M. | Galilee beach | Girl, 14, blind | Healed |
| | 9:17 A.M. | Galilee beach | Woman, 31, lame on pallet | Healed |

# JESUS' 7 MIRACLES & "I AMS"

| 7 Miracles of Jesus | 7 "I Ams" of Jesus |
|---------------------|---------------------|
| 1. Changing water into wine | 1. True Vine (John 15:1, 5) |
| 2. Healing government official's son | 2. Good Shepherd (John 10:11, 14) |
| 3. Healing disabled man | 3. Gate for the Sheep (John 10:7) |
| 4. Feeding 5,000 | 4. Bread of Life (John 6:35, 48) |
| 5. Walking on water | 5. Way, Truth, Life (John 14:6) |
| 6. Healing blind man | 6. Light of the World (John 8:12; 9:5) |
| 7. Raising Lazarus | 7. Resurrection and the Life (John 11:25) |

have life" (John 20:30–31). John put Jesus' miracles in context to show Jesus' purpose on earth—not just to heal, but to bring people back to himself. Not just to make blind men see, but to make dead men live.

John also quoted seven instances where Jesus used the term "I am." In comparing these two lists, it's apparent that Jesus wasn't talking about bread or water or light—he was talking about himself!

*9*

# The Wide-Eyed Blind Man

One of the most spectacular miracles that Jesus performed was healing a blind beggar. This was not a case of merely clearing up double vision. This man couldn't read the big *E* on the doctor's eye chart. He couldn't even see the doctor. He needed more than glasses, he needed new eyes.

Out of compassion, Jesus gave new sight to this man who had been blind from birth.[1]

Suddenly, the town beggar was walking naturally around town meeting people, walking easily without running into walls, his white cane left in the dust. He could see—no doubt about it.

So how did his hometown receive him, given his inevitable stardom? How did the press report this event?

Perhaps a local TV station would have featured the blind-man-turned-superstar in a docudrama capitalizing on his new-found notoriety. Here's a memo from TV street reporter Josephus to the program director recommending the story.[2]

# M E M O

To: Simeon, Program Director,
    WJTN (Jerusalem TV Network)
From: Josephus, investigative street reporter
Re: TV documentary on blind man "healed"
    by ex-carpenter


Facts: As you are aware, last Saturday afternoon, an out-of-town visitor named Jesus allegedly healed a blind, homeless person named Jacob who frequents the Siloam Pool. This incident has generated a flood of calls to the station seeking more information. It has also created an unexpected hostility toward Jacob by his neighbors and the Pharisees.

Proposed: I propose that we run a documentary Thursday evening during prime time. I suggest we recreate the incident to dramatize what actually happened and then use interviews with the key personalities to answer some of the questions called in to the studio, as the following storyboard shows.

---

[1]Special thanks to Donald Gass, noted ophthalmologist at the world-renowned Bascom-Palmer Eye Institute at Miami, for his medical counsel on this story. According to Dr. Gass, if a person is born blind (unable to perceive light), there is no medical cure, even with today's advanced medical technology, that can give sight, thus making the blind man's healing as much of a miracle today as it was years ago.

[2]Special thanks to Leesa Kelly, television producer in Washington, D.C., for her assistance in arranging this TV script.

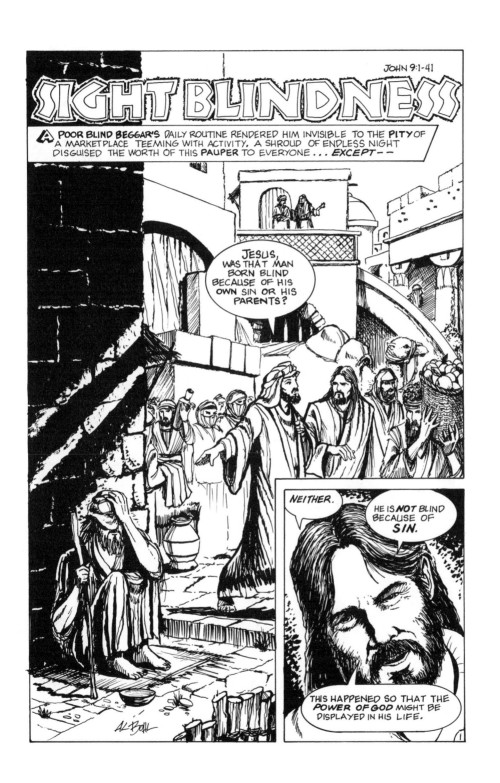

FEW NOTICED AS JESUS OF NAZARATH KNELT ON THE STREET AND **SPAT**.

HE CAREFULLY FORMED A **MASK OF CLAY**.

THE GENTLE, LOVING TOUCH OF JESUS CALMED THE FEAR OF A MAN MISTREATED ALL HIS LIFE.

GO WASH IN THE **POOL** OF **SILOAM**.

THE BEGGAR QUICKLY OBEYED THE VOICE OF THE STRANGER. HE WASN'T EMBARRASSED TO STUMBLE THROUGH THE STREET WITH MUD ON HIS FACE.

HE FINALLY FOUND THE COOL WATERS OF **SILOAM**. HE WASHED HIS EYES AND...

I...

I... CAN... SEE!

I CAN SEE!

2

A NEW MAN WALKED IN A NEW WORLD SEEING NEW WONDERS EVERYONE ELSE HAD STOPPED NOTICING DECADES AGO.

IT...**IT IS** HIM!

ISN'T THAT **TIMUS**, THE BLIND BEGGAR?

IT **LOOKS** LIKE HIM, BUT... **NO** IT COULDN'T BE.

AREN'T YOU TIMUS, THE **BLIND** BEGGAR?

YES, I AM.

WHO OPENED YOUR EYES?

A MAN NAMED JESUS PUT **MUD** ON MY EYES AND TOLD ME TO WASH IN SILOAM.

AFTER I WASHED, I COULD **SEE!**

TIMUS WAS QUICKLY TAKEN TO THE PHARISEES, THE RELIGIOUS LEADERS. THEY LISTENED CAREFULLY TO HIS STORY.

JESUS COULDN'T BE FROM **GOD.**

HE SHOWS NO RESPECT FOR THE SABBATH.

BUT HOW COULD A **SINNER** DO SUCH A GREAT **MIRACLE?**

3

THE PHARISEES DOUBTED THE MAN WAS ACTUALLY EVER BLIND SO TO BE SURE THEY SUMMONED HIS PARENTS.

IS THIS MAN **YOUR** SON?

WAS HE BORN BLIND?

HOW CAN HE NOW SEE?

THE ELDERLY PARENTS WERE ASTONISHED AND AWED BY THEIR SON, **BUT** FEARFUL OF THE JEWS. THEY KNEW THAT ANYONE WHO FELT JESUS WAS THE MESSIAH WOULD BE BANNED FROM THE SYNAGOGUE.

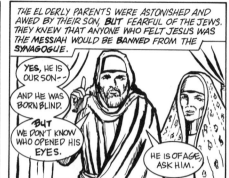

YES, HE IS OUR SON--

AND HE WAS BORN BLIND.

**BUT** WE DON'T KNOW WHO OPENED HIS EYES.

HE IS OF AGE, ASK HIM.

GIVE THE GLORY TO **GOD!** WE KNOW **JESUS** IS A **SINNER.**

I DON'T KNOW IF HE IS A **SINNER** OR NOT, BUT ONE THING I DO KNOW--

--I WAS BLIND BUT NOW I **SEE!**

WHAT DID HE DO TO YOU?

HOW DID HE HEAL YOU?

WHY MUST I TELL YOU AGAIN AND AGAIN?

DO YOU WANT TO BECOME HIS **FOLLOWERS** TOO?

WE ARE FOLLOWERS OF **MOSES!!**

WE KNOW GOD SPOKE TO MOSES, BUT WE DON'T KNOW WHERE **THIS** JESUS COMES FROM!!

4

JESUS HEARD WHAT HAPPENED TO TIMUS AND FOUND HIM.

DO YOU BELIEVE THAT JESUS IS THE MESSIAH?

YES, DO YOU KNOW WHERE HE IS?

I AM HE.

LORD I BELIEVE!

I CAME INTO THIS WORLD TO OPEN THE EYES OF PEOPLE TO THE TRUTH ABOUT GOD.

MANY WILL SEE IT, MANY WON'T.

SOME PHARISEES HEARD WHAT JESUS SAID.

ARE YOU SAYING WE ARE BLIND?!!

FAILING TO SEE TRUTH ISN'T WRONG.

REFUSING TO SEE TRUTH IS.

THE END

6

## SCENE 1—Roadside

*Interview questions for the disciples*

- Why did you ask Jesus, "Who sinned?" How could a blind infant have sinned at birth?
- Why is a deformity tied to sin anyway? Must blindness be anyone's "fault"?

*Interview questions for the blind man*

- Describe a day in the life of a blind man. What's it like begging outside the grocery? How long have you been playing the accordion?
- Describe your feelings when this mystery person put mud on your eyes. When the blinders came off.
- How many fingers am I holding up?
- What are you going to do now? Start your resume? Any movie offers?

## SCENE 2—Hometown Neighborhood

*Interview questions for the neighbors*

- How long have you known Jacob? Was he blind for all this time?
- You seem unconvinced he can see. Are you denying this?

*Interview questions for town ophthalmologist*

- When you first examined Jacob years ago, was he blind then? Can we see his charts?
- How do you explain what happened?

## SCENE 3—Synagogue

*Interview questions for Pharisees*

- You seem upset with this man. Is it because he was born blind, or because he can now see?

*Interview questions for parents of blind man*

- Where have you been all this time? Why was your son begging anyway? Why weren't you keeping him at home? Embarrassed?

*Interview questions for blind man*

- How do you feel being excommunicated? Do you feel you were better off blind?
- Have you wondered, "Why is everybody always picking on me?"

## SCENE 4—Outside the Synagogue

*Interview questions for Jesus (if we can locate him)*

- Did you really mean the Pharisees aren't seeing the truth? Aren't they more righteous than any of us?
- Why did you choose this blind man to heal?

*Interview questions for blind man*

- How do you feel now that you've seen Jesus?

# 10

# Guess Who's Coming to Dinner?

Last Monday was one of those Excedrin days I'd rather forget. I was cooped up in a smoke-filled office negotiating with four lawyers revising fine print on fine print. After ten hours straight I was exhausted, and I headed for home ready to collapse.

When I got there, Marabel reminded me of some social occasion that I had forgotten. I just wanted to relax at home, but no such luck. I hate it when that happens.

Jesus knew that feeling. One afternoon following a long day of teaching, a tired Jesus crossed the Galilee by boat. When he arrived at the other side, another large crowd gathered to meet him. Jesus then climbed a mountain with his disciples, and the people again followed.

But this time, instead of moving away, he turned to his disciples and asked, "Where will we buy bread to feed all these people?" He was more concerned about their hunger than he was his own rest.

Was Jesus asking a rhetorical question, or did he really expect an answer? Regardless, Philip blurted out, "It would take a fortune (over 200 denarii) to begin to do it."

Philip didn't believe the crowd could be fed. No way. To him it was an impossibility—a miraculous feeding wasn't among his options, and to sponsor a picnic wasn't affordable. He quickly estimated the picnic cost at 200 denarii. One denarius was one day's work, so 200 denarii represented one man's work effort for most of a year. This clearly wasn't in the disciples' meager budget.

Why did Jesus ask his original question anyway? Why didn't he just speak and produce ten zillion bag lunches? Let's roll back the conversation with instant replay.

Jesus asked, "Where will we buy bread to feed all these people?"

Philip replied, "It would cost over 200 denarii."

Wait a minute. What exactly was Jesus asking here? Didn't he just ask a "where" question, and didn't Philip give a "how much" answer? Had Philip been asked that question in court, the attorney asking the question would have repeated the question because Philip's answer wasn't responsive.

Where was Jesus heading with his question? I believe that he was entitled to something more responsive than Philip's snap remark.

Let's see how we can answer Jesus' question. Let's check with another disciple, perhaps Matthew, the former tax collector, and see how he would have tackled the project. The sheer size of the numbers involved would have certainly been a challenge to him.

---

# MEMO

TO:     Jesus
FROM:  Matthew (designated spokesman for Board of Disciples)
RE:      Food for followers

Master, when your disciples decided to undertake this project, they gave me the assignment by process of elimination. Philip was ruled out, because he had blown the answer the first time around. Peter didn't have the patience. Thomas had too many doubts. And Judas had a conflict of interest as treasurer. So the job came to me, a former tax man. (Besides, I have also had a little experience in putting on quickie dinner parties. If you'll recall when you recruited me to join your team, I got the other tax collectors together at the house on 24 hours notice. What a party! The guys are still talking about it.)

**ASSIGNMENT:** Finding food for 13,000 (approx.).

By ten o'clock this morning, a crowd of several hundred had gathered, sitting in trees and all around you as a dozen or so lame, blind, and diseased approached you. You graciously healed each one, to the cheers from the crowd.

By noon, I estimated the crowd at 3,000, with thousands more heading up the hill looking like a column of ants all the way from Galilee.

You continued your discourse until 4:30, when you took a break. By then I figure the crowd was about 13,000 people (5,000 men, 5,000 women, and 3,000 children).

You then asked us, "Where will we buy bread to feed all these people?"

**RESPONSE:** The only known food for miles around is the one sack lunch of a nine-year-old from Capernaum who has been listening to you teach since 10:00 A.M., so intently in fact that he refrained from eating his lunch for over six hours. Contents of his lunch: five small rolls and two fish.

But Master, you then added to your question, "Where will we buy bread to feed all these people?" We're talking big numbers, and for sure you're looking for more than one bag lunch.

We've checked the crowd and there's no food left. The nearest town is Capernaum, three miles away, so that's *where* we'd get food. But I think I know your follow-up questions—what kind of food, how to cook it, deliver it, and most of all, pay for it! So, I did my due diligence, and here's everything you wanted to know about food for your followers, and more!

*Menu:* What kind of food to feed this crowd? For our would-be meal, I assumed a similar fish/bread meal: mini-rolls and fish fingers.

*Food Quantities:* If a kid needs five rolls, I assume a man needs ten rolls and a woman eight. And if a kid needs two fish, give the men four fish and the ladies three. Now assuming our crowd of 13,000 starving men, women, and children, we'll need 105,000 rolls and 41,000 fish fingers.

*Production:* The next question is where to find this much food.

1. *Mini-rolls.* The nearest bakery is Capernaum Bagels, with an oven capacity of 200 rolls per load. So in order to bake 105,000 rolls, it would take 525 loads.

But how long would it take to get ready? Since the bakery is only open from 9:00 to 5:00 (closed on the Sabbath), and if it takes an hour for the bread to rise, the capacity of Capernaum Bagels is 1,600 rolls per day. That means it would take 65 days to fill the order!

By the way, this assumes that the bakery is willing to devote full-time to our one special order for the next two months and close business to its regular customers who require bread daily!

2. *Fish fingers.* Capernaum has two fish markets, Fish Aplenty, and Fresh from Galilee. If we were to buy out today's fish market supply of 300, we'd still be far short of what we need. At that rate, it would take 136 days to catch the

needed fish, again assuming that both fish markets are willing to forego their regular daily customers to fill this one special order—for 4 1/2 months!

*Packaging:* Now even if we're able to somehow get all this food at once, our next problem is packaging.

1. *Mini-rolls.* This is a huge project to box 105,000 rolls. Assume we could find some donut boxes to box a dozen each, we're talking lots of boxes—8,750 in fact. That stack of boxes would rise higher than a 218-story skyscraper.

2. *Fish fingers.* And have you ever tried to package 41,000 fish? If all these fish were laid end to end, they'd stretch almost four miles long.

If we used the same boxes for bread and fish, the stack of boxes would rise a half mile high and weigh almost twelve tons.

*Transportation:* Now even if we could locate the food and package it, how would we deliver 12,166 boxes weighing 23,625 lbs. from a village to a hillside three miles away without a road?

Very carefully, by manual transport. That means that Yours Truly and the other eleven are the logical delivery boys. But we couldn't do it all at once— each of us would have to carry a ton of food—literally!

I figure, we could each carry ten boxes and make a round trip per hour. So, at eight trips a day, with a one-hour lunch break, we could each deliver 960 boxes a day. To deliver all the boxes would take us almost two weeks!

*Cost:* If all else goes well, what will this meal cost us? When we get to the cash register, here's the really bad news:

| | |
|---|---:|
| Rolls: | |
| (105,000 at $.12) | $12,600.00 |
| Fish fingers: | |
| (10,250 lbs. at $3.00/lb.) | 30,750.00 |
| Boxes: | |
| (12,166 boxes at $.25, special order) | 3,041.00 |
| Refrigeration: | 4,000.00 |
| Baking surcharge: | |
| (for rush, extra help, etc.) | 2,500.00 |
| Storage during preparation: | |
| (three mini-warehouses) | 3,000.00 |
| Security and oversight: | 8,500.00 |
| **Total** | **$64,391.00** |

To serve 13,000 people, the net effective cost of a meal works out to $4.95 per person. This price actually seems reasonable for an All-You-Can-Eat Fish Fry, delivered. But is it affordable?

*Treasurer's Report:* For that I checked with Judas. The balance in our Disciples' Benevolence Fund is $58.45. For the rest Judas would have to check our temple line of credit.

Master, if we were to provide this one meal, it would not only clean out Capernaum, it would also clean out our treasury. The food cost would put us personally in hock for over $64,000.00, or about $5,300.00 a disciple—we who have no visible means of support. We who are worrying where we'll get *our* next meal. We couldn't even pay Judas his 45% interest!

Besides, even if we could afford this Mother-of-all-Picnics, we still couldn't get it ready and delivered for weeks or maybe months. Talk about day-old bread; we're talking petrified! And what about all that fish after a week?!

**CONCLUSION:** Jesus, this picnic isn't possible.

- Baking the bread is impossible—it would take over two months just to bake it.
- Catching the fish is impossible—it would take 4 1/2 months.
- Boxing the food is impossible—the boxes would make a stack a half mile high and weigh twelve tons.
- Transporting the food is impossible—it would take two weeks.
- Paying for the food is impossible—it would cost $64,000.00 and we're all broke.

In short, I concur with Philip—we can't afford it. Skip the meal, send the people home, and let's not worry about feeding them.

As I close my eyes, I can see Jesus reading the memo thoughtfully. I can see the disciples reading over his shoulder, nodding and expecting him to agree with Matthew's well-reasoned memo.

And then I can imagine Jesus smiling gently as he might say, "The first problem with your report, Matthew, is in your assumption that the *disciples* are to provide an all-you-can-eat fish and bagel chips dinner. You're not doing the providing—I am.

"The second problem is with your comment, 'Let's not worry about feeding them.' I never did.

"The third problem is your fear that it would take weeks to feed them. We don't have time to wait. The people are hungry now. So let's make do with what we have."

And that occasion was the origin of fast food.[1]

## Worth More Than Birds

As I finished writing this episode late one night, I flipped open my date book to glance at the next day's schedule. There, a name leaped out—a client with a difficult problem, one that had gnawed at me for six months (the problem, not the client!). I had exhausted several possible solutions that I now knew wouldn't work. But I was expected to have answers that worked, and my client's patience was in short supply. I would meet the client tomorrow.

Just then our cat, Brian, climbed onto my chair, settling down on my legal pad. Not on the empty chairs around the table, not even on the other paper piles. "Why this pad, Brian? Why?"

But as I looked at my notes next to Brian's long, slow-swishing tail, I noticed an inconsistency. While I had been writing about the disciples' lack of faith, at the same time my stomach was churning over "The Case without a Solution" I would face the next morning.

I reread Jesus' possible response to Matthew: "You aren't doing the providing—I am." And I could almost hear him say, "Charlie, you've already said you don't have the answers. Why are you worrying about this? Don't you know that I care about you? If I take care of the birds, won't I take care of you? So trust me for the answer. Let's just make do with what we have."

Brian the cat, as irritating as he can be, came along at a divinely appointed time. He changed my focus from the client's problem to the Master's solution.

Thanks, Brian, I needed that!

## When All Else Fails

If you plowed through all those statistics about delivering fish and baking bread, you deserve a reward. You must either be an accountant or a restauranteur. Congratulations on your perseverance.

For me, this exercise has shown the enormity of Jesus' miracle in feeding thousands all at once, because it would have taken this much food (or more) to feed the crowd. Talk about a mustard seed growing—this is exactly that!

What's the moral of the story? I think there are several. But one is this: A little is a lot in the hands of God. That sounds easy, but it's so hard to learn. Even the disciples who witnessed and assisted in this spectacular food multiplication had trouble learning it. In fact, not long after this event, they asked Jesus the same question—again: "Where will we get food to feed the people (4,000 this time)?" (See Mark 8:1–9.) And still later, believe it or not, after Jesus had fed 5,000 men and then another 4,000 men, the disciples were worried because they'd forgotten to bring food on a trip across the lake! (Matt. 16:8–10).

Dr. V. Raymond Edman, former president of my alma mater, Wheaton College, once said, "Never doubt in the darkness what God told you in the light."

A second moral to this story is this: Why must we exhaust all human solutions before we give God a chance to answer? A carefully reasoned solution to a given problem may leave God out of the picture, so I sometimes pray a parachute (just in case) prayer: "I've got this one covered, God, but stand by in case it bombs!" I've learned a lesson the hard way: When I'm out of answers, he's ready to help.

A third moral is: Thank God for what you have (or thank him for what you have left!). Even if you have sustained terrible loss, if you're reading this book, you can thank him for that—not the book, but your ability to read.

A fourth moral encourages an attitude of gratitude. When Jesus rang the dinner bell for the 13,000, remember the first thing he did? He asked the people to sit down—to create order and allow the people to rest. Then he said grace. He thanked his father for the food. I can picture Jesus placing his hands on that little boy's bag lunch, saying, "Let's give thanks for the food that we are about to eat."

I can picture Matthew doing a double take and whispering to Thomas, "For what?! He's giving thanks for five rolls and two fish? That won't even feed the kid! Are we all going to get one crumb? I just told him this isn't do-able! Or is he expecting Carl's Camel Catering Caravan to head up the hill any minute?"

But on that late afternoon in Galilee, with the sea glistening in the background and the sea breezes blowing, Jesus began to break the rolls and fish. Miraculously, two little fish became 41,000 fish, and five rolls became 105,000. Matthew ate until he could hold no more. So did Thomas. So did the little boy who gave his lunch and thousands and thousands more. They all left stuffed—physically and spiritually, having been fed by the Master.

That's the Savior we serve. That's the Master we follow. Nothing is impossible with him. He's bigger than the problem.

## Rainy Day Questions

1. Why did Scripture report that twelve basketfuls of food were collected after dinner? This seems like a rather insignificant aside. I mean, who keeps track of leftovers after a big party anyway? It's usually just trashed.

So who was it included? It must have been included for a reason. Were the doggie bags meant for the disciples' breakfast the next day? Or did Jesus want to demonstrate there was still food available after everyone was stuffed? Or was this an "antilitter" statement? Or a conservation lesson?

2. Do you wonder what happened when the little boy came home for dinner after being away all day long? This was not a "home alone" story, but rather an "away alone" story.

His father probably looked up from his paper and asked, "How did your day go?"

And then his mother asked, "Yes, and how was your lunch? Did you have enough?"

"More than enough, Mom," the youngster might have said. "Even shared it with a few of my friends!"

## Two Feedings: How to Throw a Picnic

If you had seen Jesus feed 5,000 men, could you ever doubt again his power to multiply food? Yet shortly after this feeding, a similar need for food arose. Compare the disciples' reaction to each occasion.

# TWO ~~FEEDINGS~~
# HOW TO ~~THROW~~ A PICNIC

| | 5,000 Men (John 6:1–12) | | 4,000 Men (Mark 8:1–9) |
|---|---|---|---|
| Jesus: | "Where can we buy bread to feed all these people?" | Jesus: | "I pity these people, for they have been here three days, and have nothing left to eat. And if I send them home without feeding them, they will faint along the road! For some of them have come a long distance." |
| Philip: | "It would take a fortune [over 200 denarii] to begin to do it!" | Disciples: | "Are we supposed to find food for them here in the desert?" |
| | | Jesus: | "How many loaves of bread do you have?" |
| Andrew: | "There's a youngster here with five barley loaves and a couple of fish!" | Disciples: | "Seven. A few small fish were found too." |
| Jesus: | Told them to sit down. He gave thanks for the food. He broke the loaves and fish. | Jesus: | Told them to sit down. He gave thanks for the food. He broke the loaves and fish. |
| Crowd: | "Everyone ate until full!" | Crowd: | "The whole crowd ate until they were full." |
| Leftovers: | Twelve basketfuls. | Leftovers: | Seven very large basketfuls. |

I don't know what particular concern might be facing you right now; only God knows that. But remember that he's the same one who fed multitudes from a single bag lunch. Remember that a little is a lot in his powerful hands.

[1]Special thanks to my friend, Charlie Olcott, former president of Burger King, for his help in planning menu portions for this exercise.

Special thanks also to John Offerdahl, former linebacker for the Miami Dolphins and now owner of Offerdahl's Bagel Gourmet, for his input concerning bagel baking.

# Part 3

# Professor Jesus
## Master Teacher

Our first recorded classroom session with Jesus was in the Jerusalem temple. Jesus was only twelve at the time. It all started when the youngster asked the rabbi a question—probably an innocent enough question, but one the rabbi couldn't answer (or ignore). The rabbi probably sought out another rabbi for help, and then there were two rabbis scratching their heads. Soon all the in-house rabbis were summoned to join the crowd of curious worshipers and puzzled rabbis.

The twelve-year-old Jesus then answered his own questions. The rabbis were amazed. It soon became apparent that the preteen interrogator knew more than the teachers. Instantly, their roles switched—tenured teachers became students, and a young student became the teacher.

Jesus became the Master Teacher from that moment on, and he continued that role throughout his life. It mattered not where he was—at a well or in a garden. Jesus would have made a good lawyer—or a good doctor or a good plumber, for that matter.

He often asked questions to open a conversation ("Will you give me a drink?"). And when others asked him questions, he often answered with a question ("Who do you say that I am?") or with a comment designed to elicit more questions of him ("You must be born again").

Jesus was available whenever people wanted to learn, and the people perceived him "as one who had great authority" (Matt. 7:29).

Jesus used familiar objects to illustrate his sermons. He was the all time greatest self-enrichment instructor. Let's look at four of his popular messages: How to Live in an Unjust World, How to Trust, How to Pray, and How to Love—God's way.

# 11

# How to Live

## Stressless Living

I had breakfast last month with John, a bank president whom I hadn't seen in months. When I asked how he was doing during these turbulent economic times, he said, "Charlie, if I could summarize my life in two words, they would be 'hurry' and 'worry.'"

He held his coffee cup in both hands as he reflected, "You know, my life is so hectic, so fast paced. I start the day before dawn and get home after dark. I have meetings almost every night. I only get to see my family on weekends, *if* I'm lucky enough to be in town. And when I'm with them, I'm worrying about the bank."

I understood John's plight. In fact, he could have been describing me as well. We were just the same, except he was a bank president![1]

As I drove to the office, I thought about his two key words: *hurry* and *worry*.

Hurry means to rush, to be fast paced, in high-speed action.

Worry, according to Webster, is from an old English word, meaning "to strangle." Worry is "an incessant attacking or goading with the intention . . . of driving one to desperation; a cause of anxiety; vexation."

Worry is the killer disease that can make a healthy man ill. Worry can paralyze a free spirit.

Jesus knew that. He had concerns too. Not about a home or wife or kids (although he had twelve overgrown, often immature kids he had to watch over!), but his responsibility was for the world—the whole world—yet not once did we see him hurry or worry.

Dr. Luke recounts an incident when Jesus addressed a group about stress. Jesus knew well the problems facing the crowd—getting a job and paying the mortgage and feeding the baby—so he gave a prescription for their anxiety attacks.

That same prescription can be refilled today. It's found in Luke 12. It's a potent remedy that doesn't cost a cent. Here's my summary of the passage.

R<sub>X</sub> **Prescription for Anxiety Attack Luke 12**

1. You are valuable to God.
   You are much more valuable than a two-cent bird (sparrow).
   He knows the number of hairs on your head (vv. 6-7).
2. Don't wish for what you don't have.
   Real life is not related to wealth.
   Jesus is not worried about money matters (vv. 13-15).
3. Don't trust in your riches, saying, "There is no problem now."
   At death, you can't take it with you.
   He is a fool who has only earthly riches (vv. 16-21).
4. Don't worry about food and clothes.
   Life consists of more than food and clothes.
   God feeds the ravens; you're more valuable than birds (vv. 22-24).
5. Worry doesn't do any good.
   Worry can't add a day to your life.
   Worry can't change small or large things (vv. 25-26).
6. Don't worry about clothes.
   God provides clothing for the flowers.
   He'll provide clothes; you're more valuable than plants (vv. 27-28).
7. Don't worry about food and drink.
   God knows your needs.
   He'll meet your needs if you seek his Kingdom (vv. 29-31).
8. Your heart is where your treasure is.
   Sell what you have and give to the needy.
   Your treasure in heaven will last (vv. 32-34).

I find at least four words or thoughts repeated in Luke 12.

1. *Don't.* The word *don't* is mentioned seven times. Jesus gave seven negative commands. Anti-commands:

- Don't wish for what you don't have (v. 15).
- Don't trust in riches (v. 21).
- Don't worry about: food and clothes (v. 23), clothes (v. 28), food and drink (v. 29).

2. *Worry.* Jesus also spoke against worry seven different times. The objects of worry? These are mainly the same ones mentioned above—food, drink, clothes, and extending life. Not much has changed since then, has it?

3. *Valuable.* The word *valuable* is mentioned four times. Jesus said that we are valuable to God:

- more than a sparrow (v. 7)
- more than a raven (v. 24)
- more than a lily (v. 27)
- more than grass (v. 28 NIV)

What connection is there between worry and security? These verses seem to tie together those two concepts. For example, "Don't worry about food and clothes. Life consists of more than food and clothes. God feeds the ravens: you are so much more valuable to him than the ravens" (see vv. 22–24).

4. *Riches.* Jesus spoke to both the rich and the rich-less, the haves and the have-nots. Regardless of your financial condition, there's a message here for everyone.

- Real life is not related to wealth (v. 15).
- Don't trust in your riches (v. 20).
- At death, you can't take riches with you (v. 20).
- It is foolish to have only earthly riches (v. 21).
- Sell what you have and give to those in need (v. 33).
- Treasure in heaven will last forever (v. 33).
- Your heart is where your treasure is (v. 34).

[1]Special thanks to John Ream, president of Citibank of Florida, who was the inspiration for this section on hurry and worry.

# 12

# How to Pray

## Prototype Prayer

Sometimes I have a hard time praying. If there's a crisis at hand, like a financial problem or surgery, then it's easy to pray. When there's nowhere else to turn, then it's prayer time—the heavy-duty, call-the-neighbors, bombard-heaven prayer time, usually reduced to one word, "Help!"

But in the routine of life, I have a hard time praying. Like this morning. I arrived at the office early before the phones started ringing. I read about Jesus healing a blind man, and then I bowed to pray.

Moments later I realized that my mind had drifted to a case I was working on. I'm not sure how long I had lapsed off, but I was embarrassed when I brought my focus back. I thought, "What if I had dozed off while meeting with a client? Or a senator? Or a king? The King of Kings!"

I went back to prayer, more earnestly this time, more focused. Within moments, my focus had again shifted. This diversion was subtle. It had sneaked in like the Stealth Bomber. Try as I would, I felt like someone else was holding the remote control, flicking my mental channels.

Jesus understood that prayer is foreign to us. How often we humans walk by sight, not by faith. Even the disciples fell asleep during Jesus' final prayer meeting. Maybe that's why he gave us a model prayer as a guide. A prototype prayer. A checklist prayer.

How do we pray, Jesus?

Thank you for the example.

# MODEL PRAYER BY JESUS

## Matthew 6:9–13 NASB

### Petitions Concerning God

| | |
|---|---|
| Our Father who art in heaven, | Preface |
| 1. Hallowed be *Thy* name, | Praise |
| 2. *Thy* kingdom come, | Petition |
| 3. *Thy* will be done, on earth as it is in heaven. | Priority |

### Petitions Concerning Man

| | |
|---|---|
| 1. Give *us* this day *our* daily bread. | Provision |
| 2. And forgive *us our* debts, as *we* also have forgiven *our* debtors. | Pardon |
| 3. And do not lead *us* into temptation, | Preservation |
| but deliver *us* from evil. | Protection |

### Praise to God

| | |
|---|---|
| 1. For *Thine* is the kingdom, | Position |
| 2. and the power, | Power |
| 3. and the glory, | Preeminence |
| forever. | Perpetuity |
| Amen. | |

# 13

# How to Trust

## Faith under Fire

Simon Peter
Galilee Docks

Dear Bertha,

Wow, You wouldn't believe what happened yesterday. It was one of those roller-coaster days.

In the morning the Master gave a great sermon. Thousands of people came—the biggest crowd I've seen around here. Looked like Jerusalem on holiday. Don't know where they all came from.

The Master was outstanding! Talked about a farmer sowing seed in four different kinds of soil and what happened to each.

The first seeds fell on a road and the birds ate them. Then some fell on thin soil with rocks beneath, but died because the roots couldn't get nourishment. Still other seeds fell among thorns that shot up and crowded out the seedlings. And the last seeds fell on good soil and grew like mad.

Then Jesus sat down. End of sermon. You could hear the crowd buzzing.

The people were surprised that he ended so suddenly. One guy near me said, "And I walked from Tiberius to hear a lecture on agriculture?!"

After the crowd broke up, I asked the Master, "By the way, Master, James didn't quite get the whole thrust of your message. Would you explain it to him?" (James didn't appreciate that one!)

Well Jesus then explained the whole nine yards to us privately. I'll show you my notes when I get back on Friday.

Then came the boat trip! It was like Mr. Toad's Wild Ride!

Jesus wanted to cross the lake. He was dead tired and needed some rest. So I borrowed Naman's boat (he had just come in and wouldn't be using it until the next morning—great guy, that Naman!), and we headed out to sea, with me at the helm.

Beautiful afternoon. Light breeze from the south, seas two to three feet. Within fifteen minutes Jesus went below and fell asleep, like a rock.

The rest of us sat around talking about how people are like soil and who fit each type. Since most of us were fishermen, the farmer stuff seemed a bit foreign, but we all figured we were the "good soil" types!

Suddenly a storm came up, within seconds, like I've never seen. A huge wave crashed over the bow, soaking us all. Then another one. And another.

This humongous storm came out of nowhere. Winds had to be fifty knots! Seas were enormous, ten to twelve feet I'd guess. We were taking on a lot of water. We tried bailing, but we couldn't stand up.

Waves kept pounding us from all sides. We were tossed like a cork, and the boat started to sink.

You know Jim and John and Andy and I have spent our lives at sea, we've fished through storms, we expect storms. But nothing like this. This was a hurricane—Hurricane Andrew, I called it, named after my kid brother.

*And then we remembered Jesus–all at once, all of us– and guess where he was? Sound asleep while we were bailing and sliding. We screamed, "Jesus, don't you care that we're about to drown?"*

*Jesus awoke (how he could sleep during the storm, I'll never know), and he looked at each of us slowly, one by one, and said, "O you men of little faith! Why are you so frightened?"*

*With that he stood up and spoke to the wind, and do you know what? The storm stopped! Immediately. As suddenly as it had started, it stopped. Not even a breeze. Unbelievable.*

*There we stood knee-deep in water looking at Jesus. I was embarrassed that I had panicked minutes earlier in front of the one who had healed lepers and fed thousands right before my eyes.*

*But I guess it was more fear than embarrassment. I was in awe of the man. And his words "Men of little faith" hurt me the most.*

*Then we started to row, mostly in silence. Without a wind, it was really tough. But suddenly, we were at the dock. We figured the Master had something to do with that too!!*

*Tell you one thing; he's the Master, and I'll never doubt him again! He's got my vote!*

*See you Friday.*

*Love,*
*Peter*

As I read the story about Peter and his pals afraid at sea, it's awfully easy to bash the disciples and think, "What's with you guys? Didn't you see him do miracles before? Didn't you know he'd protect you?"

But before I can sit in judgment on the disciples' lack of faith, I have to ask myself, "How do I respond under pressure? What is my faith factor when there's no human solution in sight? Do I panic or trust?"

# LITTLE FAITH CONDEMNED

| Problem | Reaction | Jesus' Evaluation |
|---|---|---|
| Not having the necessities of life | Fear of poverty | "Don't worry about things—food, drink, and clothes. If God cares so wonderfully for flowers . . . won't he more surely care for you, O men of little faith?" (Matt. 6:25, 30) |
| Severe storm | Fear of storms | "O you men of little faith!" (Matt. 8:26; Mark 4:40; Luke 8:25) |
| Peter drowning | Fear of sinking | "O man of little faith! Why did you doubt me?" (Matt. 14:31) |
| No food | Fear of starving | "O men of little faith! Why are you so worried about having no food? Won't you ever understand? Don't you remember at all the 5,000 I fed with five loaves and the basketfuls left over? Don't you remember the 4,000 I fed (with seven loaves) and all that was left?" (Matt. 16:8–10) (Goodness! The disciples feared they wouldn't have enough to eat even after these 9,000 were fed!) |
| Can't cast out demon | Fear of failure | "Because of your little faith [you could not drive out the demon]." (Matt. 17:20) |

In the Gospels, we have some graphic examples of Jesus' own disciples under fire, and we also have some of Jesus' on-the-spot evaluations. When they acted, he graded. Not all of these were As either. In fact, five times he gave C - grades to his own disciples for their "little faith." Not failing grades, but just barely passing!

We face these same problems and pressures today, don't we? Fear of storms, fear of failure. What if I mess up this project? What if my marriage fails? Can I recover from this setback?

It may seem that Jesus made strict evaluations in each of these examples, but notice that he was speaking only to disciples, presumably meaning, "You guys should know better by now."

### Great Faith Praised

Surely there's another grade that Jesus gives when he sees faith in action. When a person comes to Jesus for help, Jesus answers the plea, regardless of that person's level of faith. He accepts faith of any degree, even as small as a tiny mustard seed, Dijon style.

Let's look at some of the people whom Jesus said had great faith. A+ faith. Not all of these had the same amount, but Jesus commended them anyway. He met each one at his own level.

1. *Puny Faith.* When a sickly woman thought she needed to touch Jesus for her faith to become effective, it was enough. ("If I can just touch his clothing, I will be healed.") When she touched his robe, he said, "Daughter, your faith has made you well; go in peace, healed of your disease" (Mark 5:28, 34).

2. *Faith 101.* Others felt they needed Jesus to touch *them* to be healed. Their faith was dependent on Jesus' touch. A government official thought that Jesus needed to come and touch his sick child (John 4:47).

3. *Pumped Up Faith.* Others thought they only needed a word from Jesus to be healed. For example, Jesus healed a paralyzed man with just a word (Matt. 9:6–7). The man's faith was solely dependent on Jesus' word, without any touching.

4. *Creative Faith.* Some friends of a paralyzed man brought him to Jesus via a hole in the roof. They felt that because of *their* faith, Jesus would heal their sick friend. How right they were! (Mark 2:5, 11).

5. *Super Faith.* And then there was super faith—so super, in fact, that Jesus told a Roman centurion, "I haven't seen faith like this in all the land of Israel!" (Matt. 8:10; Luke 7:9).

The servant of a Roman officer was deathly ill, so the officer called the doctor—*the* doctor. The officer had probably witnessed other healings by Dr. Jesus. He knew there was no hope for his servant to live, except for a miracle. Jesus was his last resort.

So the officer asked Jesus to come to his house. I suspect that he asked something like this: "Jesus, my dear servant is very sick. The doctor has given up on him and says he's going to die. I don't want to lose my faithful servant.

"Master, I know you can heal all kinds of diseases. I saw you do it just yesterday at the park.

"I don't want to sound presumptuous, but I surely would love for you to come by my house and heal my servant. I don't want to take a lot of your busy time. It would only take a moment and . . . You would? Really? No kidding?!"

To his utter amazement, Jesus had agreed.

The officer probably did a quick mental walk-through and said to himself, "Self, now what have I done? I've invited Jesus by the house and he's coming over, right now. This busy man, this famous healer, coming by my house. Probably hundreds of people with him. Is this really necessary?"

So he probably said, "Look, Jesus, I've thought it over. On second thought there's really no need for you to stop by. You can stay here in Capernaum and just speak. I do the same thing all the time. I order things to be done and they're done. You can do the same thing right now! Just speak and my servant will be healed. I know it!"

And that very moment, in a sickbed two miles away, the officer's servant was suddenly well and leaped out of bed.

This was the gigantic faith that Jesus said he hadn't seen throughout all Israel.

Why? Because this was Long-Distance Faith. It was Reach-Out-and-Touch-Someone Faith. The officer took faith to a new level—beyond what he could see or touch. He believed that Jesus could heal an absentee third party miles away.

This is similar to what happens in a life insurance policy. If a man buys a life insurance policy on his life and names his wife as beneficiary, the contract is between the man and the company, and legally, the wife is the "third party beneficiary." She didn't pay for the policy, she didn't sign a contract, and she may not even know about the policy. But as a third party beneficiary, she can collect the proceeds at his death.

The servant boy was lying in bed deathly ill when his master was pleading with Jesus. He wasn't aware of what was going on, but through the Jesus-officer relationship, he became a third party beneficiary of his master's faith.

This concept of Long-Distance Faith has revolutionized my life. If the centurion's faith was effective to heal someone miles away, could it possibly work today? For example, if I pray for God to save a broken marriage in another state, could the Lord touch that couple as a third party beneficiary? Can I pray for a hospitalized friend in Chicago? For my daughter in Virginia? Sure I can! This is called intercessory prayer, and it's alive and well today.

6. *Blank Check Faith.* Then Jesus took the long-distance, third party prayers one step further. Shortly before he died, Jesus prayed, "I am not praying for these [disciples] alone but also for the future believers who will come to me because of the testimony of these. My prayer for all of them is that they will be of one heart and mind, just as you and I are, Father" (John 17:20–21).

Look! All believers are third party beneficiaries of that prayer. Just imagine. Not only were his prayers effective for the sick servant across town (no geographical barrier), they were also effective into the future (no time barrier), even 2,000 years into the future . . . and they're still working. This is In-Futuro Faith!

The power of intercessory prayer is greater than the power of one hundred million nuclear bombs exploding at once. Why then are we such pacifists?

## Faith Meter

| Level | Example | |
|---|---|---|
| 6<br>Blank<br>Check<br>Faith | "If we ask in his name, Jesus will answer." | Whatsoever! (John 16:24) |
| 5<br>Super<br>Faith | "If Jesus speaks, distant third person healed." | Centurion's servant (Matt. 8:10) |
| 4<br>Creative<br>Faith | "If Jesus speaks, third person healed." | Paralyzed man (Mark 2:5) |
| 3<br>Pumped<br>Up<br>Faith | "If Jesus speaks to me, I will be healed." | Man with palsy (Matt. 9:2) |
| 2<br>Faith<br>101 | "If Jesus touches my child, he will be healed." | Sick child (John 4:47) |
| 1<br>Puny<br>Faith | "If I touch Jesus' robe, I will be healed." | Sickly woman (Mark 5:28) |

How strong is your faith?
See if you can ring the bell.

# 14

# How to Love

## Loving the Unloving

When I think of Jesus' command to "Love your neighbor as yourself" (Matt. 22:39 NIV), I think of a dear neighbor of ours. His kids and ours grew up side by side. We have shared not only joys and sorrows but also tools and house keys. Loving this neighbor is an easy task. I think of him as Neighbor Love.

But then we have (or rather had years ago) another neighbor—Neighbor Not, I'll call him. The warm and friendly overtones of the word "neighbor" make it hard to call this man neighbor. Neighbor Not hated cats, specifically our cat, Sneakers. He once came to our front door armed with a shotgun and warned Marabel, "Your cat is keeping birds away from my yard. If he isn't gone by tomorrow, he'll be *gone* by tomorrow."

Unfortunately (or perhaps fortunately), I was out of town that weekend. Fortunately, my parents (a) lived three blocks away, (b) were catless at the time, and (c) were willing to suddenly adopt a cat. And (d) I have a very loving wife. I hate to think of the result if any of these circumstances had been different that day.

Anyway, Marabel quickly delivered Sneakers to her new home three blocks away, and then summoned a superhuman kindness to tell Neighbor Not, "Our cat is gone now. I'm sorry you hated her so much, but neighbors are more valuable than cats."

Neighbor Not died shortly after that. He never knew what happened to the cat, nor did he ask. Marabel, however, had put that "love your neighbor" verse into action—not just for the friendly neighbors but also for the shotgun-toting ones.

My love for others often has a direct correlation to how they love me. The Natural Love Spectrum looks something like this on a graph:

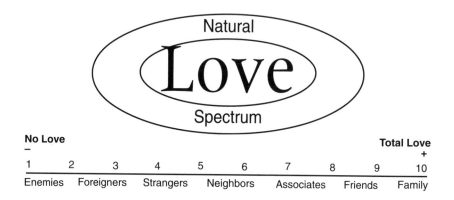

| No Love − | | | | | | | | | Total Love + |
|---|---|---|---|---|---|---|---|---|---|
| 1 | 2 | 3 | 4 | 5 | 6 | 7 | 8 | 9 | 10 |
| Enemies | Foreigners | Strangers | Neighbors | | Associates | Friends | | Family | |

And then I look at Jesus' graph. Jesus seemed to love everyone the same, even his enemies—the very ones who were plotting his death.

Jesus, who is total love himself, gave several direct commands about how and whom I should love.

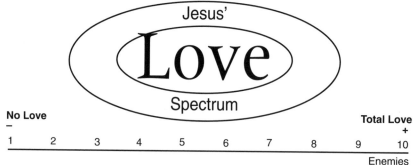

| No Love − | | | | | | | | | Total Love + |
|---|---|---|---|---|---|---|---|---|---|
| 1 | 2 | 3 | 4 | 5 | 6 | 7 | 8 | 9 | 10 |
| | | | | | | | | | Enemies |
| | | | | | | | | | Foreigners |
| | | | | | | | | | Strangers |
| | | | | | | | | | Neighbors |
| | | | | | | | | | Associates |
| | | | | | | | | | Friends |
| | | | | | | | | | Family |

1. *Love God.* The greatest commandment in the Bible according to Jesus' own words is "to love God—with 100 percent of your heart, with 100 percent of your soul, with 100 percent of your mind" (Matt. 22:37, adapted). Before talking about how to love others, Jesus wants me to focus on God with no mental reservations.

2. *Love Your Neighbor.* Then Jesus commanded, "Love your neighbor as much as you love yourself" (Matt. 22:39). (Do you think he suspected we might have problems with our neighbors?)

But Jesus, I have *two* neighbors. Which one did you have in mind? How about one out of two? Does this command apply both to the neighbor who comes with cake in hand and the other with shotgun in hand? For the ones that are hard to love, I'll have to draw on your power supply.

Another name for this Love-Thy-Neighbor law is the Golden Rule. If I am loving my neighbors (*both* of them!) as I love myself, I will do to them as I would have them treat me.

Wonder what our world would be like if everyone lived this way? How could a crime ever occur if this principle were practiced universally?

During the time of Jesus, an orthodox Jew was one who kept (or tried to keep) 613 different laws from the Torah. Of these, 365 were prohibitions like "Thou shalt not steal"—one commandment to work on each day of the year. The other 248 were mandates like "Thou shalt love the LORD thy God with all thy heart," and matched the number of bones in the human body.

The Pharisees asked Jesus, "Which of these [613] commands is the most important?" Jesus said that anyone who kept his two commands—(1) "Love the Lord your God with all your heart" and (2) "Love your neighbor as yourself"—would automatically be keeping all other commands of Scripture, for "all the other commandments and all the demands of the prophets stem from these two laws and are fulfilled if you obey them" (Matt. 22:40). Incredible. In one sentence Jesus reduced 613 laws to two!

3. *Love Your Enemies.* Jesus went further. He said to extend your love from your neighbors to your enemies. And he didn't just hit it and run, he gave four examples of how to love your enemies that hit me right between the eyes:

   a. "Love your enemies."
   b. "Bless them who curse you."
   c. "Do good to those who hate you."

d. "Pray for those who spitefully use you and persecute you" (Matt. 5:44 KJV, adapted).

That's Jesus' formula for loving your enemies—love them, bless them, do good to them, and pray for them—the LBDP formula. Wow!

4. *Love Each Other.* Finally, just before his crucifixion Jesus added yet one more command—a "new commandment" he called it. "Love each other just as much as I love you" (John 13:34).

Doug Coe, unofficial chaplain to Congress, says, "Our marching orders each day are simple—love God and love others."

So if I apply Jesus' commands to everyone, does that mean that hostile neighbors and angry customers and even strangers are to receive a ten on God's Love Scale? Sounds too good to be true. But if I love others as God loved me, then it works.

Does it work under pressure? It did for Jesus. Even while he was being murdered, he was able to forgive his very assassins. And more than that, he used the formula to forgive me! That's total love.

# Part 4

# Doctor Jesus
## One on One

Remember the *Peanuts* cartoons, the ones where Lucy stands behind a homemade wooden booth with the sign posted "Advice 5¢"?

We laugh because of what Lucy the Shrink represents. She hung out her shingle and offered her services to her playmates with problems. Lucy was a prepubertal pediatric psychiatrist.

Jesus hung out his shingle when he first announced his divinity. His humanity was already known; it was his divinity that set him apart. Troubled souls immediately recognized his counseling gifts. He was equally strong at group counseling as in private sessions. His first private patient was a nighttime appointment named Nicodemus. Jesus immediately grasped the nature of the problem, and he did it without a couch or hypnosis. He didn't charge by the hour. Jesus even undercut Lucy's nickel rate!

The prophet Isaiah wrote that the coming Messiah would be called "Wonderful Counselor." That name perfectly describes Jesus in his interpersonal dealings with hurting people. Each time Jesus counseled those suffering from guilt, depression, and grief, he furnished an appropriate response.

Never once did he turn down anyone because of gender or social status. To the contrary, many of his reported encounters were with people whom society considered outcasts.

Let's take a look at some of his other patients and see how he dealt with each one.

# 15

# Outreach to Outcasts

## Tax Collectors

During the time of Jesus, Jewish tax collectors were considered a despised class of society.[1] Why? I can think of four reasons.

*1. Tax collectors collected taxes.* Anyone who takes a portion of your hard-earned denarius can't be your friend. Who wants an involuntary business partner, regardless of the time in history? Are things any different today? When was the last time you invited an IRS agent over for dinner? In the '60s, the Beatles made popular a song called "The Tax Man," that reflects this anti-tax-collector sentiment:

> If you're drivin' a car, I'll tax the street.
> If you try to sit, I'll tax your seat.
> If you get too cold, I'll tax your heat.
> If you take a walk, I'll tax your feet.
> 'Cause I'm the tax man,
> Yeah, I'm the tax man.

*2. The taxes collected went to the enemy.* It was bad enough for Jews to pay taxes, but it was worse knowing that these taxes were going to Rome to subsidize the enemy's economy.

*3. Tax collectors were Jews.* Furthermore, each of these taxes was collected by a neighbor with whom they shopped and worshiped. Unthinkable.

*4. Tax collectors overcharged.* The final insult was knowing that the tax collectors were overcharging other Jews. They billed fellow Jews their taxes, then paid Rome its due and kept the change. Lots of it.

So is it any wonder that Jews hated the tax collectors who drove to work each day in their luxury chariots past their own neighbors who made it possible?

Enter Jesus. How did he treat this hated class? Instead of condemning them, he called one collector as a disciple and then went to his home for a private IRS dinner party. And later when Jesus spotted a second tax man, Zacchaeus, up a tree, he called him down and joined him for another IRS dinner in Jericho.

### IRS Agent Matthew

Matthew was the tax agent for the Galilee district, the popular resort area. His assignment was undoubtedly one of the most coveted in Israel. From his office he could probably see the blue-green lake and feel the gentle breezes through his open windows. He could walk along the beaches after work, fish on weekends, and enjoy a swim on hot summer days. Presumably he was a very wealthy man.

And then he met the Master, who said, "Follow me, Matthew, and I will make you a fisher of men."

Matthew instantly followed orders (he "jumped to his feet") and left his office, never again to return. Scripture reports that he hosted a dinner party in honor of his new Master and invited every tax collector around. The former tax collector became a "fisherman."

### IRS Agent Zacchaeus

When I think of the Bible story of Zacchaeus, I am reminded of a song I learned in nursery school eons ago (and still remember!):

Zacchaeus was a wee little man,
    a wee little man was he;
He climbed up in a sycamore tree
    for the Lord he wanted to see.

And as the Savior passed that way,
    He looked up in the tree.
And he said, "Zacchaeus, you come down!
    For I'm going to your house today."

Once the compact, crooked collector met the Master face-to-face, his life would never be the same. Zacchaeus promised to reform his tax collecting business, and that included giving paybacks to those he had cheated over the years. He was the same man at the same job but with a changed heart. When Jesus calls a tax collector, tax reform is at hand.

How did Zacchaeus let his customers know he had changed? The following is one man's idea of Zacchaeus's cover letter to Simon, sent out with Zack's first refund check.

---

**Zacchaeus**
Tax Agent
Internal Revenue Service
148 Main Street
Jericho

July 22, 32 A.D.

Dear Taxpayer Simon (Soc. Sec. #417-26-5347),

As you know, I have served as the Jericho tax collector for the past seven years. During that time I have collected considerable sums of taxes from you and Mildred.

Today, I am sending you a check, instead of collecting one. In fact, I am enclosing a check for 47,543.00 drachmas.

THIS IS NOT A JOKE! The enclosed check is real. It is yours. I paid it from my personal account in Switzerland. It represents the taxes that I personally overcharged you over the last seven years, times four.

So why am I sending you a refund check from my own account? And why a 400% refund?

A week ago, I wouldn't have done it, but today I'm a changed man. An honest tax collector, if you can believe that. Contradiction in terms.

It all started last Friday when Jesus was passing through Jericho. I was up a tree, trying to see over the crowd (I'm only 5'5" in sandals). Lucked out, too. When some sick, deformed, and diseased people came to Jesus, he happened to stop right under the tree where I was, so I had a good seat—or rather a good branch!

Well, in a second, Jesus healed them all. Joseph the leper, Ranan the blind guy, Sara the paraplegic.

I knew all three. I couldn't believe that I was seeing a clean leper, a blind man looking at me, and a paraplegic dancing in the streets.

I shouted down to Joseph, and that's when Jesus looked up and called my name. He invited himself over for dinner at my house. I almost fell out of the tree.

My house for dinner! My wife about died when she saw the crowd (we brought in chicken).

But afterwards, Jesus talked with me. Just the two of us. I realized that this man is the Messiah.

Simon, something special happened to me that day. I became a new person. I told Jesus I was a lousy guy and a cheat on the job, but I planned to give half of my property to the homeless on Temple Terrace. In addition, for those I had cheated, I promised to give back 400%.

That's the purpose of this letter. I hope you understand what I'm saying, but more than that, I hope you understand my new Master.

Very truly yours,
Zacchaeus

P.S.: You can ignore the special Sidewalk Lantern Assessment I sent you Tuesday.

# TWO TAX COLLECTORS

| Matthew | Zacchaeus |
|---|---|
| *Reference:* (Mark 2:13–17)<br>*Position:* Tax collector at Galilee beach (aka Levi, son of Alphaeus) | *Reference:* (Luke 19:1–10)<br>*Position:*<br>1. Very influential<br>2. Very rich<br>3. Very short |
| *Setting:* Jesus walking at the beach, saw Matthew sitting at his tax collection booth. | *Setting:* Jesus passing through Jericho, city below sea level, deathly hot. Crowds around Jesus. Zacchaeus ran ahead, climbed sycamore tree beside road to watch. |
| *Jesus' Command:* "Matthew, Come with me. Come be my disciple." (Follow me) | *Jesus' Command:* "Zacchaeus! Quick! Come down! For I am going to be a guest in your home today!" |
| *Matthew's Response:*<br>1. Jumped to his feet and went along. (Matthew the disciple)<br>2. Invited fellow tax collectors for dinner with Jesus and disciples. (Matthew the missionary)<br>3. Quit his job. | *Zacchaeus's Response:*<br>1. Hurriedly climbed down.<br>2. Took Jesus to his house with great excitement and joy.<br>3. Reformed his life.<br>  a. Pledged to give 50 percent of his wealth to the poor.<br>  b. Pledged to penalize himself by refunding 400 percent to anyone he overcharged on taxes. |
| *Reaction of Guests:*<br>1. Notorious sinners and tax collectors came and many believed.<br>2. But some Jewish religious leaders (uninvited) said, "How can he stand it, to eat with such scum?" | *Reaction of Crowds:*<br>Displeasure. "He has gone to be the guest of a notorious sinner." |
| *Response of Jesus:* (Overhearing remarks of religious leaders) "Sick people need the doctor, not healthy ones! I haven't come to tell good people to repent, but the bad ones." | *Response of Jesus:* "This shows that salvation has come to this home today. . . . I, the Messiah, have come to search for and to save such souls as his." |
| *Matthew's Career Plans:* Left his job, followed Jesus. | *Zacchaeus's Career Plans:* Went back to work a changed man, now an honest tax collector. (Not an oxymoron!) |

### Two Officials

Whenever Jesus reached out to heal, he did so without regard to age or race or social status. He even reached out to government officials and soldiers of the enemy Roman army. Compare Jesus' dealings with each.

# TWO OFFICIALS

|  | Government Official (Jewish) (John 4:46–53) | Soldier (Roman) (Matt. 8:5–10) |
|---|---|---|
| Location: | Cana | Capernaum |
| Initial Request to Jesus: | 1. "Come to my house" (in Capernaum twenty miles away), he begged.<br>2. "Heal my son" (who was near death's door). | 1. "Come to my house," he begged.<br><br>2. "Heal my servant boy" (who was paralyzed and racked with pain). |
| Jesus' Response: |  | 1. "I will come<br>2. and heal him." |
| Acknowledgment: |  | 1. "I am not worthy to have you in my home."<br>2. "It isn't necessary for you to come." |
| Second Request to Jesus: | "Sir, please come now before my child dies." | "If you will only stand here and say, 'Be healed,' my servant will get well! I know you have authority to tell his sickness to go—and it will go!" |
| Jesus' Response: | 1. To the crowd (with disappointment), "Won't any of you believe in me unless I do more and more miracles?"<br>2. To the government official:<br>　a. "Go back home." (He did, believing.)<br>　b. "Your son is healed!" | 1. To the crowd (with amazement): "I haven't seen faith like this in all the land of Israel!"<br><br>2. To the Roman officer:<br>　a. "Go on home." (He did, believing.)<br>　b. "What you have believed has happened!" |
| Result: | Boy was healed that same moment. | Boy was healed that same hour. |

### Two Adulteresses

John records two incidents involving Jesus with women of ill repute. Yet there was no scandal on his part nor any falling to temptation—only Jesus' compassionate heart, which resulted in two changed women.

# TWO ADULTERESSES

|  | Samaritan Woman at Well | Jerusalem Woman at Temple |
| --- | --- | --- |
| *Reference:* | John 4:4–30 | John 8:1–11 |
| *Parties:* | Jesus and woman (alone) | Jesus and woman (crowd) |
| *Setting:* | Well; open air, noonday heat | Temple; Jesus mobbed by throng, Pharisees and leaders |
| *Woman:* | Known adulteress | Caught in act of adultery |
| *Opening Question:* | Question by Jesus, "Will you give me a drink?" | Question by Pharisees to Jesus, "Moses' law says to kill her. What about it?" |
| *Jesus Identifies Sin:* | "You have had five husbands, and you aren't even married to the man you're living with now." (He identified *her* sin.) | Stooped down and wrote in dust with his finger. "He who is without sin, let him cast the first stone!" (He identified *their* sin.) |
| *Jesus' Lesson:* | His living water endures more than water from a well. | All have sinned. |
| *Response:* | She:<br>1. Left her water pot beside well to follow Jesus as a disciple.<br>2. Went back to the village and told everyone (as a missionary). | Jesus' command to the woman: "Go and sin no more." (Jesus neither condemned the woman nor condoned her sin.) |
| *Result:* | A changed woman | A changed woman |

[1]Special thanks to Terry Crook, a Florida IRS collection agent (no kidding, an honest crook!), for her input concerning tax collectors.

[2]Special thanks to James Towey, Florida State Director of Health and Rehabilitative Services (HRS), for his insight on dealing with "outcasts." One of the main functions of the HRS office is to aid those that society rejects—the homeless, the terminally ill, the indigent, etc. Towey, having worked with Mother Teresa in India and in an AIDS shelter in Washington, D.C., brings a compassionate heart to a sometimes dispassionate bureaucracy.

# 16

# Outreach to Kids

## Disciples' Bulletin

### For those attending Jesus' lecture today

Welcome to today's lecture by Jesus. He will probably start speaking at 9:30 A.M. But before he does, I'd like you to meet him and his team.

First there's Jesus. For those of you hearing him for the first time, here's a little bio on him:

- Ex-carpenter from Nazareth
- Now lives in Capernaum when he isn't on the road
- Amazing lecturer
- Can heal (and has healed!) the diseased and the lame and the blind. Keep your eyes peeled at all times.

Then there's us. We call ourselves the Disciples. We're the ushers in the yellow T-shirts. There are twelve of us, if you're counting.

My name is Judas. I'm the treasurer of this group. As one of the Disciples (Jesus' advance team), I have traveled with him since he started his speaking tour. In recent weeks very large crowds have turned out to hear Jesus, and I expect another big one today. Because of this, I (or rather we the Disciples) have established some guidelines today to provide for your comfort and convenience. Please observe the following:

Page 2

Crowd Control Guidelines
1. Bring your own lunch. No food will be provided.
2. If you have small children, babysitting is provided by the big oak tree (ten drachmas/hour), or sit in the back with your kids. Please don't let them distract Jesus.
3. Please observe the Special Seating Sections as provided on the signs and stay within the ropes of your section:

   · Disciples—front rows reserved
   · Friends and family of disciples—next ten rows
   · Galileans—next thirty rows
   · Open seating section in the middle
   · Wheelchair section next to road
   · Back rows—lepers, Samaritans, tax collectors, prostitutes, and all others

**Seating Arrangement**

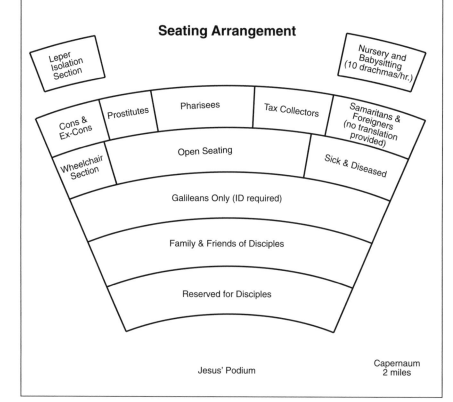

Leper Isolation Section

Nursery and Babysitting (10 drachmas/hr.)

Cons & Ex-Cons | Prostitutes | Pharisees | Tax Collectors | Samaritans & Foreigners (no translation provided)

Wheelchair Section | Open Seating | Sick & Diseased

Galileans Only (ID required)

Family & Friends of Disciples

Reserved for Disciples

Jesus' Podium

Capernaum 2 miles

Marabel and I were in a packed theater last week when a little girl behind us started to cry. We (along with 200 other angry patrons) said, "Shhh!" in unison and tried to block out the unwelcome sounds.

That same frustration probably motivated the disciples to keep children away from Jesus. Who could tell when some screaming meemie would let loose during Jesus' message? Children's behavior can't be predicted—but then neither could Jesus'.

And Jesus, had he picked up one of these handouts,[1] would have probably said, "No, Judas. Let the little children come to me, and do not hinder them, for the kingdom of heaven belongs to such as these" (Matt. 19:14 NIV, adapted).

> Jesus loves the little children,
>   And the lame,
>     And the lepers,
>       And the sinners.
> Whosoever will, may come.

Jesus came to take the ropes down.

### Jesus Loves the Little Children

Jesus was a magnet drawing children to him. He loved them and they loved him. Look at how many times he focused his attention on young people.

#### He Healed Kids

- Government official's son in critical condition. Jesus healed him (John 4:46–53).
- Twelve-year-old daughter of Jairus. Jesus touched her corpse at her home and raised her (Mark 5:35–43).
- Young man at Nain. Jesus touched the coffin on the way to the cemetery and raised him (Luke 7:11–15).
- Girl at Tyre. Her mother asked in faith, so Jesus cast out a demon (Mark 7:25–30).
- Boy. His father had asked in faith, so Jesus cast out a demon (Mark 9:14–29).

#### He Protected Kids

Jesus protected the faith of little children and warned against anyone tampering with that simple, innocent faith: "If any of you causes one of these little ones who trusts in me to lose his faith, it would be better for you to have a rock tied to your neck and be thrown into the sea" (Matt. 18:6).

### He Identified with Kids

Jesus said, "Whoever welcomes a little child like this in my name welcomes me" (Matt. 18:5 NIV). "And if, as my representatives, you give even a cup of cold water to a little child, you will surely be rewarded" (Matt. 10:42).

What a promise—bless a child and you're blessing Jesus!

### He Revealed Truth to Kids

Jesus prayed, "Thank you for hiding the truth from those who think themselves so wise, and for *revealing* it to little children" (Matt. 11:25, emphasis added).

Out of the mouths of babes comes special truth from the very heart of God. Listen carefully when children speak and consider the source.

### He Selected a Boy's Lunch to Multiply

Jesus fed 5,000 men from a boy's bag lunch instead of sending the crowd home hungry.

### He Provided Angels for Kids

"Don't look down upon a single one of these little children. For I tell you that in heaven their angels have constant access to my Father" (Matt. 18:10).

That information shouldn't come as a surprise to parents who see their young children dodge danger daily. How else but through angels' watchful care could they be kept safe?

### He Honors Kids' Faith

Jesus said, "If a child asks his father for a loaf of bread, will he be given a stone instead? If he asks for fish, will he be given a poisonous snake? Of course not! And if you hardhearted, sinful men know how to give good gifts to your children, won't your Father in heaven even more certainly give good gifts to those who ask him for them?" (Matt. 7:9–11).

In his best-selling book, *All I Ever Really Need to Know I Learned in Kindergarten,* author Robert Fulghum wrote, "Life could be so less complicated if we all went back to our kindergarten roots:

Share everything.
Play fair.
Don't hit people.
Put things back where you found them.
Clean up your own mess.
Say you're sorry when you hurt somebody.
When you go out into the world,
Watch out for traffic, hold hands, and stick together."

Jesus added one more maxim to the list when he admonished some adults, "Become as little children, [or] you will never get into the Kingdom of Heaven" (Matt. 18:3).

As I reread those words of Jesus, I wondered why he said, "Become as little children." Why didn't he hold up some other individuals as role models, like Pharisees or doctors or teachers? Why children, of all people?

One Sunday morning at church I was talking with some friends and their third-grade son, Hal. I thought, "This is my chance to ask a child what Jesus meant by that comment." I leaned over and said, "Hal, I want to ask you a question. Jesus told some people one day, 'Unless you become like a little child, you won't get into heaven.' What do you think he meant by that?"

Without a moment's hesitation Hal said, "Oh, that's easy. It's only when you're a child that you really know what's going on!"

I thought to myself, "He's probably right." Then I asked him, "Do you think that children have more faith than adults?"

His eyes looked up as he thought and then said, "Ummm, I don't know. I've never been an adult before!"

Wow! He had it. That's it. Little children are so spontaneous in their faith. Through the eyes of a child, life is simple. It's when we become mature and sophisticated that we can miss the simple plan he intended for us.

That's why Jesus said the road to God leads through kindergarten!

---

[1]Special thanks to Ralph Sanchez, president of the Miami Grand Prix, for his suggestions concerning crowd control at open-air events.

# 17

# Sister Act

The tale of two sisters story as told in Luke 10 immediately follows the good Samaritan passage and precedes the Lord's Prayer. Why is this story of two sisters and their spat even included in the Bible? And why is it sandwiched between the good Samaritan and the Lord's Prayer? A sister spat between two classics. Why?

Mary and Martha, together with Lazarus, their brother, were close friends of Jesus. They lived in Bethany, a suburb of Jerusalem. Their home was apparently open to Jesus on short notice to eat with them, weep with them, and speak powerful personal words to them. The two sisters are mentioned by all four gospel writers in three different episodes.

## 1. The Dinner (Luke 10:38–42)

Martha was the Martha Stewart of her day, the household hostess and party planner extraordinaire for weddings, bar mitzvahs, and other celebrations.

On one special night, however, her guest of honor was the Guest of Guests, the most honorable of all. She greeted the Master and no doubt quickly tried to count the extra guests he had brought with him. Mental note: "Next time remember to send out RSVP cards."

Martha rushed into the kitchen to prepare the meal but soon realized that Mary wasn't helping. Looking back toward the others, she saw Mary at Jesus' feet, listening while he taught.

Imagine Martha's feelings. Here she was, frazzled by the sudden company, while Mary was relaxed, drinking in the Master's words.

In exasperation (probably after trying to catch Mary's attention), Martha interrupted Jesus' discourse. "Sir, doesn't it seem unfair to you that my sister just sits while I do all the work? Tell her to come and help me."

I can imagine the awkward silence in the room as everyone awaited Jesus' reply.

Then he spoke to her, ever so gently. "Martha, dear friend, you are so upset over all these details! There is really only one thing worth being concerned about. Mary has discovered it—and I won't take it away from her!"

(Note: Scripture does not record whether Martha ever served dinner, but knowing Jesus' ability to provide meals on short notice, I doubt whether anyone went home hungry that night.)

---

*Mary—will you get in here and do your kitchen duties I need you now!!!— Martha*

**Checklist**
**Dinner with Jesus and Friends**
**Friday night**

**To Do:**

| | Mary | Martha |
|---|---|---|
| 4:00 P.M. | Sweep floor | Put pies in oven |
| 5:00 P.M. | Peel potatoes | Set up hors d'oeuvres |
| 7:00 P.M. | Serve cider | Kitchen replenish |
| 7:25 P.M. | Serve hors d'oeuvres | |
| 7:30 P.M. | Serve dinner | |

---

### 2. The Funeral (John 11:1–44)

Lazarus had been sick for two weeks and was now near death. His sisters, Mary and Martha, sent an urgent message to Jesus: "Sir, your good friend is very, very sick."

This was a 911 emergency call, time for sirens, speed, and flashing lights.

But Jesus, upon receiving the message, was not in a hurry. Instead he stayed two more days before heading to Bethany.

By the time he arrived, Lazarus had already died, four days earlier. Friends and family had stopped by to console the sisters.

Martha greeted Jesus angrily, "Sir, if you had been here, my brother wouldn't have died." When Jesus told her that Lazarus would rise from the dead, Martha snapped, "Yes, when everyone else does, on Resurrection Day." And when Jesus ordered the gravestone rolled away, she protested: "By now the smell will be terrible, for he has been dead four days."

Mary, on the other hand, after showing initial dismay over Jesus' late arrival, began to weep and fell down at Jesus' feet. This is the same place we last found her at the dinner party weeks before.

Jesus wept too. But tears of sorrow were short lived as Jesus said those still-reverberating words, "Lazarus, come out!" And suddenly a corpse was walking. Now tears of joy abounded as Mary and Martha embraced their resurrected brother.

### 3. The Anointing (John 12:1–11; Matt. 26:6–13; Mark 14:3–9)

Jesus knew that his time had come. He would be on earth only one week more, and he spent one of his last dinners at the house of Simon the ex-leper. Jesus' other friends were also included—the Twelve, Martha, Mary, and Lazarus.

What do you think that dinner conversation was like? I think that someone probably asked Simon to tell about life as a leper, and I can imagine his story. "My house was defiled, condemned, and off-limits. No one came within a hundred yards. Even the mailman left my mail under a rock down the road. When I left home to beg, passersby walked a wide path around me, some throwing stale food or coins. I couldn't receive any medical treatment. No one approached me except other lepers . . . and Jesus.

"But *now!*" the ecstatic Simon blurted out, "here we are at dinner! This is my first home-cooked meal and you're my first guests."

Then undoubtedly Simon told of that momentous day, how Jesus entered Jerusalem and laid his healing hands on the emaciated beggar with open sores.

"Suddenly," Simon shouted, "I was healed! My leprosy was gone. I had new skin everywhere. I was a new man!"

As the cheers went up, it was Lazarus's turn. Not as a "Can you top this?" competition but rather as a supportive sharing of praise. Lazarus probably told of the sickness, his final memories, and then loss of consciousness. "I don't remember a thing after that until I heard Jesus shout, 'Lazarus, come out!'

"The next thing I remember is jumping up and then falling over in some mummy outfit. I couldn't stand up. I didn't know where I was. Everything was dark. All I could do was groan until you rolled me across the room, unwrapping me. Look, I've still got tape in my hair!"

And I imagine more hugs and tears and cheers for Lazarus, as friends and family witnessed this death-to-life, walking/talking miracle.

It may have been Mary who then turned to Jesus and implored, "Teach us, Master." Jesus probably paused a moment, and then he began to tell of his impending death. It was almost time. This would be one of his final messages—words of comfort and hope. Special words.

I can see Mary quietly and inconspicuously leaving the room, then returning with a flask of perfume. Without a word, she gently poured the fragrant essence on his head and feet and, having no towel available with which to dry them, wiped them with her hair.

The disciples watched the intimate ceremony. Jesus ceased his discourse.

Then an exasperated Judas broke the silence. "Why, she could have sold that perfume for a fortune and given the money to the poor."

Can't you imagine the righteous glare in Jesus' eyes? Can't you see him placing his hands on Mary's moist hair and reassuring her with a loving look?

"Leave her alone," he told Judas. "Why berate her for doing a good thing? You always have the poor with you, and they badly need your help, and you can help them whenever you want. But I won't be here much longer. Mary has done what she could, and has anointed my body ahead of time for burial. And I tell you this in solemn truth, that wherever the Good News is preached throughout the world, this woman's deed will be remembered and praised."

It is easy to identify with these sisters because we all encounter the same topics daily—fixing dinner, family arguments, unfairness, deadlines, party planning, anger, grief, and joy.

*Martha.* Martha's the one we love to pick on. She was generous, gracious, and outgoing, with a take-charge personality. She was a gourmet cook and extremely organized.

Her weaknesses? She was a perfectionist and expected others to agree with her agenda. She was overly concerned with details, even if it made others around her feel uncomfortable. She feared that the meal might not measure up to her expectations. She hoped that Jesus would say, "What a great meal—the best one I've had since the Galilee Gourmet!"

Martha didn't handle stress well. She was impatient. When Mary refused to help in the kitchen, Martha got madder by the minute—banana peel by banana peel, cheese blintz by cheese blintz!

When I read this story of the sisters, I asked myself:

1. Can getting caught up in the details of life make me forget the big picture?
2. Is there a proper time to listen to Jesus and a proper time to work for him?
3. Can serving Jesus keep me from worshiping Jesus?

Jesus said it best: "Martha, you are worried about many things. There is only one thing worth being concerned about and Mary has discovered it."

*Mary.* Then there's Mary. There's no doubt that she loved Jesus dearly. She had the gift of hospitality; she knew how to make a guest feel welcome. She would rather talk (or listen) than cook. She was more interested in the guests' words than the cleanliness of the house or the promptness of the meal. She wanted a home more than a house. She was a responder.

Jesus' evaluation of Mary? "She has discovered what really matters. She has done what she could. . . . Wherever the Good News is preached throughout the world, this woman's deed will be remembered and praised."

Which epitaph would you want on your tombstone? "She was upset over many things" (Martha), or "She has done what she could" (Mary)?

Which sister loved Jesus more? Maybe they both loved him the same, but Mary's actions were highlighted by Jesus—the listening, the worshiping, and the anointing, all at the feet of Jesus. That must be where it all starts.[1]

[1]Special thanks to my daughters, Laura and Michelle, the joys of my life—both of whom are "Marys"!

# A Tale of Two Sisters

| | **Dinner with Jesus** (Luke 10:38–42) | **Lazarus's Death** (John 11:1–44) | **The Anointing** (John 12:1–11; Matt. 26:6–13; Mark 14:3–9) |
|---|---|---|---|
| *Sisters' Actions:* | Martha greeted and cooked—workaholic. Mary sat at Jesus' feet. | Martha greeted. Mary fell down at Jesus' feet. | Martha served dinner. Mary anointed Jesus' feet. |
| *Complaint:* | *Martha:* 1. "Jesus, doesn't it seem unfair that my sister sits while I do all the work?" 2. "Tell her to come and help." | *Martha:* 1. "Sir, if you had been here, my brother wouldn't have died." 2. "By now the smell will be terrible, for he has been dead four days." | *Judas:* "That perfume was worth a fortune. It should have been sold and the money given to the poor." |
| *Jesus' Response:* | *To Martha:* "You are so upset over all these details. You are worried about many things." *To Mary:* "There is really only one thing worth being concerned about. Mary has discovered it—and I won't take it away from her!" | *To disciples:* "Roll the stone aside." | *To Judas:* 1. "Why berate her for doing a good thing?" 2. "She has done what she could." *To all:* "Wherever the Good News is preached throughout the world, this woman's deed will be remembered and praised." |

# Part 5

# A Day in the Life of Jesus

## Jesus' Date Book

# 18

# How to Deal with Interruptions

## Roller Stone

### Jesus: A Day in the Life

#### by James bar-Gephas

It's a long way from a Nazareth carpentry shop to a mountainside teeming with humanity. Oh, it's just a few miles as the arrow flies, but the career of Jesus of Nazareth has been just that—an arrow shot straight into the beating, bleeding heart of Galilee.

Who is this Jesus? And what made him set foot on this rocky road of celebrity?

He's a Rabbi-with-a-Difference, to be sure. His teachings sing with the sweet sound of making sense, a noticeable change from the fol-de-rol that Caiaphas and Company have been dishing out. The "love your neighbor" shtick is nothing new, really. It's the "love your enemy" business that knocks our socks off.

But this rabbi is a rabble-rouser, and the crowd around him on this morning is anxious for change.

9:45 A.M. I'm with him on a mountainside in Galilee, one of those grassy rolling hills that slopes gently into the azure sea. But the slope is a sea of people right now. Faces everywhere, all trained intently on the one who is training them, this swarthy, bearded carpenter who is driving nails through their assumptions and building a new container for truth.

He is seated, rabbi-style, and his cadre of aides forms a standing semicircle behind him. They are almost a Greek chorus, framing the central action, which is of course Jesus.

I sit off to the side, with a handful of other reporters. Andrew Barjona, Jesus' press secretary, looks over at me nervously every few minutes, hoping I'll spin this article positively. I don't think he has anything to worry about—with a crowd like this, my spin won't matter much. They are drinking it all in.

Jesus tells a story, another one, this one about two men who build two houses—one on sand and one on rock. You can see this punch line coming from across the lake, but the people are nodding and smiling. The teacher's voice thunders with the account of an approaching storm, and the crowd seems to shudder a bit. They've seen squalls roll in off the lake. And guess what? The house on sand collapses while the house on rock stands. "Build your house on the rock of my teachings," Jesus concludes, and he stands up. The sermon is over. Go home now.

But they don't. They stay to watch what this rabbi does next.

10:15 A.M. Jesus talks with his aides and then walks down the mountain toward Capernaum Road. The crowd parts like the Red Sea, each face gazing adoringly. His smile seems to take in each person and comfort them, yet without words.

At the base of the hill, where road meets sea, Jesus is approached by a man in rags. The crowd gasps, "It's a leper," probably escaped from the colony on the other side of the hill. One of Jesus' henchmen darts forward to intercept this interloper, but Jesus waves him off. The man kneels and asks for healing—"That is," he stammers, "i-if y-you want to."

You could cut the crowd's silence with an oar as Jesus reaches out to the outcast. "I want to," he says. "Be healed." He touches the man on his scabby cheek. Grateful, the now healed man runs off.

Oh, yes. Did I forget to mention this other thing that Jesus does? He heals people.

# Page 3

11:17 A.M. An hour later, Jesus enters Capernaum. The crowd behind him seems even larger than on the hillside. A Roman centurion, decked out in full military duds, rides up on horseback. "Uh-oh," the crowd murmurs. Jesus is going to get it now. Parading without a permit, or some other half-cocked infraction invented by Roman bureaucrats with too much time on their hands.

But the centurion dismounts and kneels before Jesus. "My servant is ill and needs your healing," he begs.

Jesus helps the captain to his feet and commands, "Show me where you live. We'll go there."

"No!" the captain protests. "I don't deserve to have you under my roof. Just say the word, and my servant will be healed."

Jesus comments on the faith of this Gentile, then sends some healing vibes in the direction of the centurion's house.

11:33 A.M. Andrew Barjona is handing out press releases on the next day's itinerary when his brother Peter sidles up to him. Peter, many say, is Jesus' right-hand man, but he doesn't seem to be exulting in the glory of the moment. He whispers to Andrew that his mother-in-law is very sick. Andrew says, "Let's tell the Master."

Jesus is playing skip-stones with children in a poor section of Capernaum. The kids seem to be enjoying this new game, and Jesus is pretty good at it too. Andrew and Peter interrupt him with news of Peter's mother-in-law. In a moment, Jesus hands his last stone to a nearby child and heads off with Peter to do another healing.

11:47 A.M. Acting press aide Andrew explains that the press will have to wait outside as Jesus tends to Peter's mother-in-law. The crowd has thinned some, as people have returned to their daily work, but there are still fifty or sixty people packed into this narrow street, waiting for Jesus to emerge again.

1:15 P.M. The doors open and Jesus' aides bring some food out to the waiting crowd. The old woman is all better and has been cooking up a storm. I gobble up the best smelt dumpling I've ever had.

3:07 P.M. I'm about to pack it in. It's been a long day, but Jesus is still at it. He has set up just outside of town, and a long line of people with various ailments is winding down the road. Every time I look, the line is longer. There are people hobbling on crutches, being carried on beds, dancing in a frenzied agitation, howling in demonic rage. One by one, group by group, they approach the healer, who deals with what ails them.

3:48 P.M. I can see from his face that Jesus is growing weary. His aides move down the line to explain that Jesus will not be doing any more healing today (their idea, not his). Maybe tomorrow. There is disappointment on many faces, but a seeming acceptance. Beggars can't be choosers. Hopes dashed today can be reborn tomorrow, especially when you've had a lifetime without hope.

4:15 P.M. "Let's cross the lake," Jesus says, and several aides hurry off to prepare the boat. There are several fishermen in Jesus' inner circle, Andrew tells me. They know the lake well.

But as Jesus sets off for the seaside, he is interrupted once again, this time by one of the yuppie lawyers from central Capernaum. He has several men and women with him, upper-crust folks who've been doing some "slumming"—hiking out to the burbs to see the miracle worker put on his show.

The man seems truly moved by what he has seen. His companions seem surprised as he steps toward Jesus. "Teacher," he says, "I want to follow you. I'll go anywhere."

Jesus looks long and deep into this man's eyes, as if measuring his soul. He then launches his baritone voice louder than necessary so that everyone hears—his aides, those who had been healed and those who hadn't, the young lawyer and his cohorts. "Foxes have holes to live in, and birds have nests." He then gestures to himself, "But the Son of Man has no place to lay his head."

One of the lawyer's companions calls, "I'll follow you too, but I have to bury my father first."

The woman next to him laughs and elbows him. "But your dad isn't dead yet," she whispers.

Jesus fixes his gaze on the whole group of them. This is serious stuff now. The laughing Jesus who played skip-stones with little kids is now a stern Jesus who needs to make his point. There is a frightening power in his countenance. "Follow me," he thunders. "And let the dead bury their own dead."

The yuppie group slinks away, back to their posh lodgings, as Jesus heads for the lake. His work for the day is not yet done. There are miles to go before he sleeps.

Whenever I become distressed over the interruptions of life, I am reminded that Jesus' life was filled with constant interruptions. His date book did not contain a series of scheduled appointments from nine to five, but rather he met people where they were and he dealt with them as they came to him. He was available, never too busy to lend a hand.

Of course, a skeptic might say, "Well, that was easy for Jesus! He didn't have anything else to do. He didn't have to worry about holding down a job, or taking care of a family, or making mortgage payments." Maybe not, but on him were the pressures of the entire world, since that was his mission in life.

Life is the art of improvisation, and Jesus proved that he was able to cope with life's distractions as they arose.

How then did he deal with interruptions? Look in Matthew 8 at his Day-Timer for a typical day in Galilee. He preached on a mountain comparing himself with Moses. Then he came down the hill with the crowd following.

*Interruption 1:* A leper asked to be healed and instantly was cured of the deadly disease.

*Interruption 2:* He was then intercepted by a Roman centurion who said that his servant was critically ill and asked Jesus to come to his house to heal him. Jesus agreed to make the detour, but once Jesus did, the centurion said that it would not be necessary if Jesus would only speak a word long-distance. The servant was instantly healed, and the centurion's faith was commended.

*Interruption 3:* Jesus then received notice that Peter's mother-in-law was critically ill. He made his way to the house and brought her back to life and health.

*Interruption 4:* Leaving the house, some demon-possessed people screamed at Jesus, and he took time to heal them. Jesus told his disciples, "Get the boat ready. We're going to cross the lake."

*Interruption 5:* Before reaching the boat, a Jewish leader stopped him for a time of questioning in front of the people.

*Interruption 6:* Before Jesus could board the boat, one would-be disciple said, "Excuse me, I will be glad to follow you under certain conditions. I will be available as soon as my father dies." And then he turned away. A very tired Jesus got into the boat to begin crossing the Sea of Galilee. Within minutes, he was asleep.

*Interruption 7:* A violent storm arose.

*Interruption 8:* The disciples screamed for Jesus to save them. Jesus awoke and spoke the words, "Peace, be still." The seas obeyed.

*Interruption 9:* When the boat arrived on the other side, Jesus was ready to rest, but instead, he was met by two demon-possessed men who met the boat screaming. He dealt with the men and cast the demons into some pigs, which charged into the sea and drowned.

*Interruption 10:* Jesus was still looking to rest, but the townsfolk were so upset about losing their pigs, they said, "Get out of here." They kicked him out of town. So Jesus joined his disciples back at the boat and crossed back to Capernaum.

*Interruption 11:* When he stepped on shore, he was met by a boy who was paralyzed. Jesus healed him.

*Interruption 12:* Jesus then saw Matthew, the tax collector, and called him to follow him.

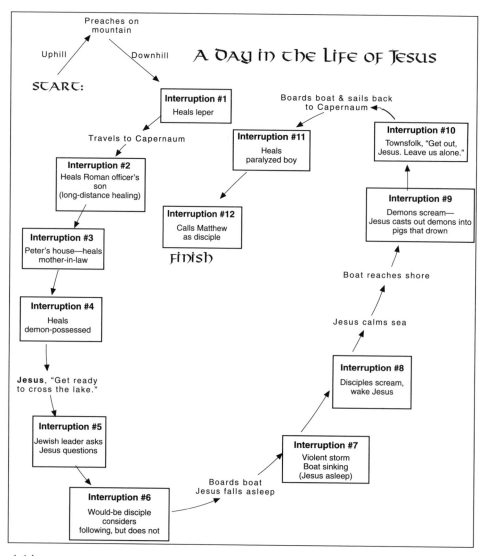

How could a day in the life of Jesus be summarized?

1. Teaching to multitudes
2. Healing a leper
3. Healing paralysis
4. Raising Peter's sick mother-in-law
5. Healing demon-possessed
6. Confronting Jewish leaders
7. Calling a man to discipleship (chose not to follow)
8. Lake crossing for rest and relaxation
9. Riding out a hurricane
10. Calming a hurricane
11. Exorcising two more demons
12. Wiping out one herd of pigs
13. Being forced out of town for wiping out the bacon business
14. One more lake crossing
15. Another paralysis healing
16. Calling another man to discipleship (chose to follow)

It is interesting to note that not one of the events of this particular day in Jesus' life was a scheduled appointment, each one appeared as an interruption. Or were all of these events part of his divine schedule?

What does that say to us? How do we deal with distractions? Are we too busy with our daily schedules to have time for the sidelights of life, which may be divine appointments? Perhaps that's why Jesus said, "Do not worry saying, 'What shall we eat, or what shall we drink, or what shall we wear?'" (Matt. 6:31 NKJV). Or whether we make every appointment exactly as scheduled.[1]

[1]Special thanks to Dick Capen, U.S. Ambassador to Spain and master of improvisation, for his personal example and guidance on how to handle interruptions.

# 19

# Artist of Word Pictures

## Show-and-Tell Time

I was in fifth grade when I first heard the word "parable." A gray-haired Mrs. Webster was discussing various figures of speech and telling me far more about each one than I cared to know. Besides, at 2:00 P.M., with only an hour to go, I had already put my brain in neutral. As I heard her announce a pop quiz late one Friday afternoon, I thought, "It's not fair and I don't care!"

Looking back, I wish I had cared, especially when I read the parables of Jesus. I have had to do some latter-day cramming since grade school to catch up on my grammar, but I think I finally figured out figures of speech, umpteen years late. And in case you were sleeping in that same fifth-grade class, I'll share my notes with you on figures of speech—four of them:

1. *Simile.* A simile is a figure of speech in which a thing or action is compared, usually with the words "as" or "like." We hear these similes all day long:

He's tough as nails.
She's smooth as silk.

He's solid as a rock.
The baby's cries are like music to her ears.
She's like a sister to me.

The prophet Isaiah used a simile when he wrote, "All we like sheep have gone astray" (Isa. 53:6 KJV).

Jesus himself said, "How often I have wanted to gather your children together as a hen gathers her chicks beneath her wings" (Matt. 23:37).

2. *Metaphor.* A metaphor is another figure of speech literally describing an object or an idea in place of another to suggest a likeness. A metaphor is a stronger description than a simile. Instead of using a simile "He's like a rock," the metaphor is "He *is* a rock." Or "She's an angel," "He's a crybaby," "He's history."

Martin Luther used a metaphor for the title of his majestic hymn, "A Mighty Fortress Is Our God." Jesus used a metaphor when he told believers, "You are the light of the world."

3. *Allegory.* An allegory is an extended metaphor. For example, Jesus said, "I am the true Vine and you are the branches" (a metaphor by itself), but then he expanded on this word picture to make it into an allegory. He talked about bearing fruit, pruning vines, and being fruitful vines, all in a spiritual sense.

He used other allegories when he proclaimed, "I am the Resurrection and the Life, the Good Shepherd, and the Bread of Life," and then he amplified what each one meant, turning metaphors into parables.

John Bunyan wrote his great masterpiece, *Pilgrim's Progress,* as an allegory of a pilgrim searching for the meaning of life.

4. *Parables.* A parable is an extended simile. It tells an earthly story with a heavenly meaning. Jesus started with a simile when he said, "The kingdom of heaven is like a tiny grain of mustard," but then he elaborated. That extended simile became the parable of the mustard seed.

---

**Figures of Speech**

Simile ("as" or "like")  → becomes  Parable (an extended simile)
Metaphor ("is")  → becomes  Allegory (an extended metaphor)

---

Gospel writers Matthew, Mark, and Luke record Jesus' parables, while the Gospel of John records the allegories stemming from the seven "I ams" mentioned by Jesus.

A parable is a story that compares the familiar with the unfamiliar in order to teach some higher spiritual truth. In the Greek, *para* means "beside" (from which we get our word *parallel*). *Bal* means "to throw" (from which we get our word *ballistic*). Thus *parable* means "to throw beside," one meaning beside another.

Jesus began teaching by parables only after the religious leaders rejected him. He told his disciples that he would reveal certain secrets of the kingdom of heaven to them, but not to the religious leaders (Matt. 13:11), and that this knowledge would remain obscured to those who did not believe.

For example, when Jesus said he was the Bread of Life, some listeners took him literally, asking, "How can this man give us his flesh to eat?" Their spiritual blindness kept them from seeing the deeper, spiritual application of the story that compared manna (bread) with his body, as bread that would be broken for them. So they left bewildered, wondering what was so profound about the bread story.

What if Judas (ever thinking how he might turn a quick buck) had tried to publish Jesus' parables? This is what the publisher's reply letter might have looked like.[1]

---

# *People's Press & Scrolls*

### 317 Main Street
### Tiberius

Mr. Judas Iscariot
Galilee Docks
Capernaum

Re: "Jesus Parables" Manuscript

Dear Mr. Iscariot:

We received your letter of June 7th and the collection of 27 stories told by Jesus, your leader. As the New Scrolls Editor, this manuscript was referred to me for review.

Having heard about Jesus (but never meeting him personally—just missed his temple lecture in Jerusalem last month), I read his stories very carefully.

His tales are fascinating, without a doubt. He's quite a storyteller. But frankly, these stories ("parables" as you call them), don't seem to fit the guidelines for our Great Classics Series, for several reasons:

1. Some parables are too short. For example, the Mustard Seed story is only one paragraph long. It's not long enough for a good chapter and wouldn't even fill a page. It's as tiny as a mustard seed (pardon the pun). Not much substance to the story unless your teacher could expand it.

2. Other parables are pointless. That is, they have no lesson, no moral. Take, for example, the Lost Coin story. A lady lost a coin, so she searched for it and found it. End of story. Big deal. People lose coins and find coins every day. It's just not worth a lot of hype. What's the significance in finding a coin?

And on top of that, the follow-up story about finding a lost sheep is redundant. "Deja vu all over again," to quote a famous disciple.

Perhaps you could group these stories together under a title like "Lost and Found Department" or "The Fervent Seeker," but there's still no point to the whole thing. We don't want to insult our readers' intelligence (or our editor's!).

3. Other Jesus stories seem to be aimed at special interest groups—like tax collectors and farmers and even "foolish virgins." In publishing a book, it's important to first define your market and then stay with it. If we published this book, bookstores wouldn't know whether to carry it in the Fishing Section or the Construction Section or the Bridal Section. Perhaps you can get your teacher to narrow his focus and quit spraying his topics. Just who is he speaking to, anyway?

4. Probably the biggest drawback to the Pilgrim's Parables is the negative message some of them send.

Take the Lost Sheep story for example. Some farmer hires a kid to guard his 100 sheep. One sheep strays away. So what does the kid do? Protect the 99? Nope, he goes looking for #100, and when he finds it, he's praised for it.

What message does this story send to other shepherds? Protect your flock, your 99 sheep? No, instead leave what you've got for sure to search for what you may never find. When the shepherd gets back with the one, the other 99 may be lost or stolen or may have wandered away.

Pure poppycock. Tell your master to change this ending. Tell him it's far better to protect the 99 woolies.

Remember the old drinking song:

99 woolies all safe in the fold,
  99 woolies all safe.
If one of those woolies should happen to stray—
  98 woolies all safe in the fold.

The Good Samaritan story is another example of a negative lesson taught through parables since Jesus is urging people to stop and help stranded travelers. Has Jesus been on another planet? Hasn't he read about our runaway crime wave? The smash and grabbers? The camel-jackings? Suggest to Jesus that he stress self-defense! When passing someone in distress don't even slow down! Remember, it could be a trap.

And finally there's the Prodigal Son story, where the delinquent takes his inheritance and blows it in grand style. Then he comes crawling home wondering if his father would let him work as a servant.

The message from Jesus? The father not only welcomes him, but he kisses him and forgives him. He restores him to the family. He even throws a huge party, kills the fatted calf, and clothes him with new shoes, a new ring, and, get this, a new robe. Hardly a proper message for kids about to leave home.

If I were the father of this kid, I'd slam the door on him. The last thing a no-good punk needs is forgiveness and love. Tell Jesus he'll have to learn about the real world. Tell him it's a dog-eat-dog world out here.

Judas, thanks again for thinking of us. Let us know if you get any more hot book ideas. I suggest you keep a diary of your travels, and if you ever leave the "fold," we could do an exposé on the whole Jesus movement.

Just a thought.

Very truly yours,

*Abimilech*

Abimilech, New Scrolls Editor

Matthew reported, "Jesus constantly used these illustrations when speaking to the crowds. In fact, because the prophets said that he would use so many, he never spoke to them without at least one illustration. For it had been prophesied, 'I will talk in parables; I will explain mysteries hidden since the beginning of time'" (Matt. 13:34–35).

Jesus used at least forty parables to teach his disciples. His most frequent topics were money (nine parables), labor relations (eight parables), and agriculture (six parables), and he also used other familiar objects and events like parties, fishing, cattle, and housing.

Perhaps the most universally known parable of Jesus was the parable of the prodigal son, where the delinquent son returned home and, instead of being treated as a servant, he was treated as the guest of honor.

What son could leave such a loving father in the first place?! It makes us wonder, until we realize how often we do the same thing to our heavenly Father. But no matter how gross our rejection, he's still watching and waiting for our return.

[1]Special thanks to Alvah Chapman, chairman of the Executive Committee of Knight-Ridder Publishers, for his suggestions concerning publishers' rejection letters, and for his encouragement throughout the writing of this book.

THE YOUNG MAN FLASHED HIS CASH AND QUICKLY FOUND FLASHY FRIENDS, FLASHY GIRLS, FLASHY CARS, AND FLASHY FUN.

SET 'EM UP, BARTENDER, DRINKS ON ME!

JOE, BUDDY, CAN YOU SPOT ME A THOU·?

YOU BET, ARE YOU SURE THAT'S ENOUGH, PAL?

SIGN HERE AND THE BRIDGE IS YOURS.

COOL!

JOE, I LOVE DIAMONDS!

JOE IS GREAT!

NEEDLESS TO SAY, HIS MONEY WAS GONE IN A FLASH.

JOE, YOU'VE RUN UP QUITE A BILL HERE AT THE HOTEL. IT'S TIME TO SETTLE.

MR. THOMAS, I'M A LITTLE SHORT, CAN YOU GIVE ME SOME TIME.

BILL

MR. THOMAS DIDN'T LIKE THE IDEA.

HIS NEW FRIENDS DISAPPEARED AS FAST AS HIS MONEY. HE THOUGHT ABOUT JUMPING OFF THE BRIDGE HE BOUGHT, BUT HE COULDN'T LOCATE IT. THE ONLY JOB HE COULD FIND WAS FEEDING PIGS.

TASTES DRY, BUT IT'S FOOD!

HEY, THAT'S MINE!

I WONDER HOW MY FAMILY IS DOING TONIGHT?

EVEN MY FATHER'S SERVANTS HAVE FOOD.

2

JOE WAS ASHAMED OF HOW HE HAD WASTED HIS INHERITANCE. HE KNEW HE HAD BECOME A DISGRACE TO HIS FAMILY. HE WAS SURE THAT HE WASN'T WORTHY TO BE HIS FATHER'S SON.

I'M GOING HOME. MAYBE I CAN BE A SERVANT TO MY FAMILY.

DAY AFTER DAY JOE'S FATHER WATCHED THE HORIZON. HE WASN'T SURVEYING HIS WEALTH, HE WAS HOPING TO SEE HIS SON RETURN.

IS THAT MY SON COMING? IT IS MY SON!

THE RICH MAN DIDN'T WAIT FOR HIS SON TO COME TO HIM. HE RAN FROM HIS MANSION AND UP THE DUSTY ROAD TO MEET HIS WAYWARD SON.

FATHER, I AM SO SORRY, I WASTED EVERYTHING YOU WORKED SO HARD TO GIVE ME.

I AM NO LONGER WORTHY TO BE YOUR SON.

PLEASE LET ME BE YOUR SERVANT.

NO MATTER WHAT, YOU ARE MY SON.

WE MUST CELEBRATE YOUR RETURN.

THE RICH MAN ORDERED HIS SERVANTS TO PREPARE A GREAT BANQUET IN HONOR OF HIS SON.

THE IMPORTANT THING IS THAT YOU CAME HOME.

MY SON WAS DEAD AND NOW HE'S ALIVE!

HE WAS LOST, BUT NOW HE IS FOUND!

I DON'T DESERVE THIS PARTY. I HAVE BEEN AN EMBARRASSMENT TO EVERYTHING YOU STAND FOR.

THE END

3

# 20

# Team Disciples

Jesus called twelve young men as his special followers. Most were fishermen who left everything to follow him. They became his "team"—Team Disciples, you might call them.

Team Disciples soon discovered that this team would be going on the road—a lot. They began to travel with their leader in the cities, in the country, and on the beach. As a group they faced the crowds, both friendly and hostile.

What kind of men were Jesus' disciples? Did holy living come naturally to them? Were they yes-men who liked to play follow the leader? Did their lifestyles match the sacred titles that we ascribe to them today—titles like Saint James, Saint Peter, and Saint Thomas— or were they free spirits, each with a mind of his own? Were they tempted as other men, and did they fail as other men?

Fortunately, the Bible depicts the disciples as mortals, subject to the same frailties that beset disciples today. Peter's walking on water is recorded, but so is his sinking from lack of faith. This most vocal disciple both defended Jesus with a sword and, hours later, denied him with an oath.

Does that surprise you? Or disappoint you? Wouldn't it have been prettier to have excluded the downfalls? Perhaps, but for me, it's encouraging to know that this ragtag bunch isn't a team of Super Saints. In fact, a review of their lives shows them to be members of the "Yo-Yo Gang"—up and down, up and down.

Let's take a closer look at the team in action.

# THE DISCIPLE SERIES
# TRADING CARDS
*Now available for the first time!!*

**All Rookie Set**

*The Dream Team!*
*Start your collection TODAY!!*

## Meet the Disciples up close and personal!
You've seen 'em in the park!
You've seen 'em on the beach!
You've seen 'em in the stores!

## Now take them home with you—
## your very own set!

These cards are sure to increase in value!
Pick up an extra set to laminate.

*Personally autographed sets available.*
A written certificate of authenticity
provided with each autographed set.
Trades for silver and perfume considered.

# LIVING LEGENDS
Contact: Judas
P.O. Box 30
Tiberius
*Dial* 1-800-NEW-TEAM!

## DISCIPLE SERIES

### Bartholomew
### "Nathanael"

Famous Blooper Quote: "Can any good thing come out of Nazareth?"
Only disciple to hesitate when called.
"One in whom there is no guile." Jesus

## DISCIPLE SERIES

### Matthew
### "Levi"

College major: Finance.
Former Tax Collector in Capernaum (retired).
On Top 10 Most Wealthy Galileans List.
Unpopular; keeps to self; few local friends.
Excellent number-cruncher.
Abandoned profession when called by Jesus.
Hobby: Writing - keeps diary of Jesus' travels.

DISCIPLE SERIES

THADDAEUS

## DISCIPLE SERIES

# Thaddeus
# a/k/a/ Judas
# (Not Iscariot)

His only recorded question to Jesus
- "Why reveal yourself only to
followers and not to the world?"
Good listener.
A man of few words.

DISCIPLE SERIES

SIMON

## DISCIPLE SERIES

# Simon the Zealot

Former member of extreme radical,
revolutionary party
Fiercely patriotic and loyal.
Roommate Matthew - though
politically opposite; called the
Odd Couple.
Doesn't take "no" for
an answer.

## DISCIPLE SERIES

THOMAS

## DISCIPLE SERIES

### Thomas
### "The Twin"

Has twin brother.
Intensely loyal - "Let's go too -
and die with him (Jesus) Jn. 11:16.
Given to skepticism: a cynic.
Chmn., Medical Confirmation
Committee
Refused to accept excused absence
when a disciple called in sick;
insisted on doctor's letter. Demands
proof; has mind of a scientist.
Favorite saying: "I doubt it!"

## DISCIPLE SERIES

JAMES

## DISCIPLE SERIES

### James
### Son of Alphaeus
### "The Lesser"
### "Little Jim"
### "Shorty"

Friend of Zacchaeus
(both 5'2")
Wears platform sandals.
Voted: "Most Likely to Have
an Inferiority Complex" in
high school.

## Simon Peter
## "Rocky"

Former fisherman, left huge catch
to follow Jesus.
Roomate - his brother Andrew
Quick tempered, impulsive.
Makes rash promises.  Member
of 3-Man Executive Committee.
Promises total loyalty to Jesus.
Self-proclaimed spokesman for
group.

## James
## Son of Zebedee

Part of "Sons of Thunder" Group.
Member of 3-Man Executive Committee.
Extremely ambitious.
Mean streak - asked Jesus to call
down fire on Samaritan village.
Roommate: Brother John.
Voted: "Most Likely to Succeed"
at Galilee High.

DISCIPLE SERIES

JUDAS ISCARIOT

DISCIPLE SERIES

## Judas Iscariot

Ambitious.

Ruthless.

Treasurer (self-appointed).

Working on Fund Raising Manual.

Only disciple with summer home and boat.

Voted "Most Willing to Sell His Grandmother Down the Pike" in high school.

DISCIPLE SERIES

ANDREW

DISCIPLE SERIES

## Andrew

Former disciple of John the Baptist until John said "Behold the Lamb of God".

Former fisherman until Jesus said "Follow me."

1st to believe in Jesus.
1st disciple of Jesus.
1st to bring another to Jesus.
(Peter)
1st missionary.
Uniform #1

## DISCIPLE SERIES

### John
### "The Love Bug"

Former commercial fisherman in Galilee.
Member of 3-Man Executive Committee.
Member of "Sons of Thunder" Group.
Ambitious - usually sits near Jesus.

Good listener - takes good notes of Jesus' sermons.
Voted: "Mr. Congeniality" in High School Class.

## DISCIPLE SERIES

### Philip

Former commercial fisherman in Galilee.
Was fishing while "caught" by Master Fisherman.
Closest friend - Bartholomew (whom he brought to Jesus).
Has a questioning nature - asked Jesus about feeding 5,000.
College major: Pre-law.

### Foot-in-Mouth Disease

Throughout their travels, the disciples weren't always convinced. Sure, they loved their leader, but privately they wondered whether he could fully take care of himself and, more important, them.

So often this Yo-Yo Gang acted more like the Faithless Flock than Team Disciples. Over and over we read of their gaffes. Here are some sound bites from the disciples over three brief years with Jesus. Some of these comments show a stubborn ignorance of Jesus' identity and mission. Some were undoubtedly quotes they wished they could have taken back.

"Who is this, that even the winds and the sea obey him?" (Matt. 8:27).

"Why do you always use these hard-to-understand illustrations?" (Matt. 13:10).

"It is already past time for supper, and there is nothing to eat here in the desert; send the crowds away so they can go to the villages and buy some food" (Matt. 14:15; Mark 6:36).

"We have only five loaves of bread and two fish among the lot of us, or are you expecting us to go and buy enough for this whole mob [of 5,000 men]?" (Luke 9:13; Matt. 14:17; John 6:7–9).

"It would take a fortune to buy food for all this crowd!" (Mark 6:37).

"You offended the Pharisees by that remark" (Matt. 15:12).

"Tell her to get going, for she is bothering us with all her begging" (Matt. 15:23).

"And where would we get enough here in the desert for all this mob [of 4,000 men] to eat?" (Matt. 15:33).

"Are we supposed to find food for them here in the desert?" (Mark 8:4).

"[Children,] don't bother him [Jesus]" (Matt. 19:13).

"Teacher, don't you even care that we are all about to drown?" (Mark 4:38).

"All this crowd pressing around you, and you ask who touched you?" (Mark 5:31).

"Then who in the world can be saved, if not a rich man?" (Mark 10:26).

"Are you really the Messiah? Or shall we keep on looking for him?" (Luke 7:18).

"Master, shall we order fire down from heaven to burn them up [the Samaritans]?" (Luke 9:54).

"This is very hard to understand. Who can tell what he means?" (John 6:60).

"Master, why was this man born blind? Was it a result of his own sins or those of his parents?" (John 9:2).

"Master, only a few days ago the Jewish leaders in Judea were trying to kill you. Are you going there again?" (John 11:8).

"Let's go too [to Lazarus]—and die with him" (John 11:16).

"What a waste of good money. Why, she could have sold it for a fortune and given it to the poor" (Matt. 26:9; John 12:5).

"Master, shall we fight? We brought along the swords!" (Luke 22:49).

And then there was Peter, the most outspoken of the merry band. Though he would later became a leader of the disciples, he had more than his share of bloopers.

"Heaven forbid, sir. This is not going to happen to you [you will not die and rise again]!" (Matt. 16:22).

"Sir, it's wonderful that we can be here! If you want me to, I'll make three shelters, one for you and one for Moses and one for Elijah" (Matt. 17:4).

"We left everything to follow you. What will we get out of it?" (Matt. 19:27).

"You shouldn't say things like that" (Mark 8:32).

"Oh, sir, please leave us—I'm too much of a sinner for you to have around" (Luke 5:8).

"Lord, how many times shall I forgive my brother when he sins against me? Up to seven times?" (Matt. 18:21).

### Jockeying for Position

During his final days on earth, Jesus held private meetings more frequently with his disciples. He was preparing them for his death and their coming persecution. At the same time, they were scrambling for the best seats available, much like ringside seats at a big prize fight.

The disciples asked Jesus who would be the greatest in the kingdom of heaven (Matt. 18:1).

James and John asked him, "Master, we want you to do us a favor. We want to sit on the thrones next to yours in your kingdom, one at your right and the other at your left!" (Mark 10:35, 37).

The mother of James and John brought her sons to Jesus and asked for a favor: "In your Kingdom will you let my two sons sit on the thrones next to yours?" (Matt. 20:20–21).

At dinner, the disciples tried to sit near the head of the table by Jesus (Luke 14:7).

The disciples argued among themselves who would have the greatest rank in the kingdom (Luke 22:24).

### Trite Questions at the Final Meal

What if you had been invited by Jesus Christ to his final dinner party, and when you arrived, you were among only twelve honored guests? If Jesus had opened the conversation by telling about his imminent death, what questions would you have asked when he was finished? Deep theological questions about the end times, or questions about his suffering?

Fortunately we have the actual recorded conversations of what the disciples asked. Listen to their remarks around the table.

1. *Who's the greatest?*
   The disciples: "They began to argue among themselves as to who would have the highest rank" (Luke 22:24).
2. *Wash my feet?*
   Peter: "Master, you shouldn't be washing our feet like this!" (John 13:6).
   "You shall never wash my feet!" (John 13:8).
   "Then wash my hands and head as well—not just my feet!" (John 13:9).
3. *Will I betray you?*
   Each of the disciples: "Am I the one [to betray you]?" (Matt. 26:22).
   Judas Iscariot: "Rabbi, am I the one?" (Matt. 26:25).
   Peter: "Ask him which one he means" (John 13:24 NIV).
   John: "Lord, who is it?" (John 13:25).
4. *Where are you going?*
   Peter: "Master, where are you going?" (John 13:36).
   "But why can't I come now? For I am ready to die for you" (John 13:37).
5. *Deny you?*
   Peter: "If everyone else deserts you, I won't" (Matt. 26:33).
   "Lord, I am ready to go to jail with you, and even to die with you" (Luke 22:33).
   "No! Not even if I have to die with you! I'll never deny you!" (Mark 14:31).
6. *What's going on?*

Thomas: "We haven't any idea where you are going, so how can we know the way?" (John 14:5).

Philip: "Sir, show us the Father and we will be satisfied" (John 14:8).

Judas (not Iscariot): "Sir, why are you going to reveal yourself only to us disciples and not to the world at large?" (John 14:22).

The disciples: "Whatever is he saying? What is this about 'going to the Father'? We don't know what he means" (John 16:17–18).

The disciples: "At last you are speaking plainly, and not in riddles" (John 16:29).

### Jesus Who?

Jesus predicted that his own disciples would abandon him. "But the time is coming—in fact, it is here—when you will be scattered, each one returning to his own home, leaving me alone" (John 16:32).

Hours later this prophecy came true. When Jesus was arrested, the disciples fled, possibly to the same upper room with doors locked (Matt. 26:56; John 20:19).

Even Peter the Lionhearted became Peter the Chicken Liver. He managed to follow Jesus at a distance, but when onlookers challenged Peter on his association with Jesus, the Rock became the Wimp—three straight times.

"I don't even know what you are talking about" (Matt. 26:70; Mark 14:68; Luke 22:57).

"I don't even know the man" (Matt. 26:72; Mark 14:70; Luke 22:57).

"[I swear] I don't even know the man" (Matt. 26:74; Mark 14:71; Luke 22:60).

But after Jesus returned from the dead a dramatic transformation took place. Look how Peter and the gang reacted. Faith finally took hold in that upper room where Jesus and the disciples had both their final communion and first reunion.

Thomas initially doubted, but when he was confronted by the living Jesus, he cried out, "My Lord and my God!" (John 20:28).

Peter told Jesus, "You know I am your friend . . . Yes, Lord, you know I am your friend . . . Lord, you know my heart; you know I am [your friend]" (John 21:15–17). Jesus showed forgiveness and compassion, even though Peter had denied him.

## The Rest of the Story

Later, the remaining eleven disciples scattered across the known world spreading the gospel, no longer huddling together for safety or even for fellowship. Judas, of course, never made it out of Jerusalem (see Matt. 27:3–10).

Some of the disciples then wrote several books of the Bible. John wrote five books: the Gospel of John, three letters bearing his name, and Revelation. Matthew, aka the Evangelist, wrote the Gospel of Matthew. Peter wrote two letters bearing his name and was probably the major source behind Mark's Gospel.

During Jesus' final hours, the disciples ran away together, hid together as cowards. But after Pentecost, empowered by the Holy Spirit, they could stand courageously. According to tradition, every one of the Eleven, except for John, died as a martyr for his faith in Christ. John was exiled for his faith but died a natural death on a rocky island.

# 21

# Night Fishing with Captain Peter

Simon Peter was a fisherman long before he was a disciple. If he was anything like the Florida fishermen I know, fishing was more than a business. It was his life, his passion.

When Peter first appears in Luke's Gospel, he is beside his boat, washing his net. He had been fishing all night but hadn't caught anything. Jesus came by and Peter's luck changed. You could say his whole world changed.

Boating was second nature to him. He spent hours at sea, not only because he loved to fish but also to put bread, or rather fish, on the table.

One unique feature about Peter's fishing—he often fished at night, all night. He left the docks at dusk and returned at daybreak.

It was only fitting that Peter the Fisherman should first meet Jesus the Carpenter by the sea—and after a night of futile fishing, at that.

So how did Peter in one twenty-four-hour period return to the docks both empty-handed and with his largest catch ever?

Listen to his story as it might have been told to reporter Sara—a story of overcoming in the face of adversity, a story of hope in the midst of despair. Peter's story is a lesson for anyone who has ever been frustrated.

# How the Empty-Handed Fisherman Caught Fish

Peter's new boat, *Night Stalker*, glistened as it glided slowly toward the Galilee dock at 8:00 A.M., a bit later than its usual daybreak return. The other boat crews impatiently waited for the current fishing report from Peter before casting off.

Peter's night-fishing exploits were known around the lake, but no one really knew his fishing techniques because he fished under cover of darkness. Perhaps the fish feed better at night, yet the other fishermen were unwilling to sacrifice their sleep for that possibility.

"How'd you do, Pete?" one asked the uncharacteristically quiet Peter.

"No good," yelled Peter. "Shut out."

"Shut out?! You? Pete, you haven't been shut out in ten years. What did you do all night, take a nap?"

Peter shrugged his shoulders and said, "I don't know. I tried everything. Go get 'em. I left a lot out there."

And the rest of the fishing fleet headed out to sea.

As Peter tied up the bow line, he sorted out his feelings. It had been a long, pitch-black night at sea, and Peter didn't need any more snide remarks.

He was hungry. His shoulders ached from casting nets for twelve hours straight. His lower back hurt, causing great pain when he turned. He hadn't slept since early yesterday afternoon. Every nerve of his body cried out for sleep.

He thought, "Fishing is a funny business. Here I've worked hard all night while these guys slept, but they'll probably be back before noon with a full boat of fish. Meanwhile, I've got no fish to sell, but I have to pay my crew, the dock rent, and the boat payment. I should have kept the old boat. I never got shut out on it."

Just then a voice interrupted. "Hey, mister. How come you're not going out with all those other boats?"

"I've already been out," he started to explain but then thought, "Why try?"

"I'm going out later," he sighed, and that seemed to satisfy the lad's curiosity.

13

Peter looked up the hill and saw a large crowd heading toward the dock. He asked the youngster, "What's going on up there?"

"Oh, it's Jesus. We've followed him from Capernaum."

Peter saw a man in a white robe, with his back to the water addressing the crowd in a semicircle around him. Several hundred.

"So that's Jesus," Peter thought. "Jesus the miracle worker, healer, and teacher of truth. Super Rabbi."

Jesus turned and walked toward the sea with the crowd following. Peter arranged his nets so he could clean out the seaweed while he listened to Jesus' strong voice now within earshot, amplified by the crystal smooth sea.

"He's coming this way," Peter thought, his heart racing. "Closer now. My word! He's heading right for me. He's looking right at me!" Peter's eyes met the rabbi's loving eyes, understanding eyes.

Before Peter could utter a sound, Jesus reached the boat and stepped aboard. Peter was speechless. Imagine, Jesus in sandaled feet, on board the *Night Stalker!*

In a firm voice Jesus said, "Peter, push off shore a bit."

A startled Peter replied, "Yes, sir," and his hands fumbled as he untied the bow line, trembling with excitement and wondering how Jesus knew his name. "Have we met somewhere before?" he thought.

At about twenty feet from shore, Jesus said, "That's enough," and he sat down and faced the people on the docks and hillside. Peter dropped the anchor. He was the only one on board, with the best seat possible, as he sat and listened, spellbound.

Jesus had seen a tired and discouraged Peter and singled him out. Was it a coincidence that the most popular person in all of Israel should single out Peter's smelly fishing boat for his pulpit? Or did Jesus plan it all?

"If only I'd known," thought Peter. "Why didn't I clean the boat before cleaning the nets?" But Peter's thoughts were soon focused on Jesus, as he heard the Master teach wonderful truths about life.

By noon, the message was over. How time flew. The crowd dispersed but the Master remained to talk with Peter. No one else. Just Peter.

Peter didn't feel tired any longer. His back spasm had gone, and he looked in awe at his most memorable guest ever.

Jesus looked directly into his eyes and said, "Put out into deep water. Let down your nets for a catch." The sole passenger had given the captain instructions a second time.

Peter was startled at how quickly Jesus had changed subjects from loving one's neighbor to instructions about fishing. Peter thought, "What does this stranger know about fishing? Sounds a bit presumptuous to tell the top Galilee fisherman how to fish, doesn't it? Why the deep water? Why another fishing trip after an all-nighter? It's time for bed."

But Peter remembered that the

14

Master had assured him a result—he would catch fish. The command was really a condition—"*If* you go into deep water and lower your nets, you *will* catch fish."

Peter, unable to resist, blurted out, "Master, I've worked hard all night and caught nothing," which was his most tactful way of saying, "I've already tried that—for the past twelve hours. I know it's not going to work; it's not humanly possible."

But as his heart responded to those loving eyes of the Master looking deep into his own, he reversed himself in mid-sentence and said, "Nevertheless, because you say so, I will let down the nets."

That morning, Peter caught such a large number of fish that his nets began to break, and he had to signal another boat to come help. The fellow fishermen came and filled the boats so full they both began to sink.

The record catch was greater than anything Peter could have expected—the largest catch of his life, on a day when he would have been grateful for a sardine for breakfast.

He fell at Jesus' feet and said, "Go away from me. I am a sinful man." In the presence of God, Peter realized his unworthiness.

Jesus extended a most unusual invitation to Peter, "Follow me, and I will make you a fisher of men."

Peter pulled his boat ashore and followed him. Peter left everything—his boat, his dock space, his career, his means of support, even his greatest catch ever. He left all to follow Jesus.

## Galilee Revisited

Three years later, after Jesus' resurrection, the grieving, guilty, and confused Peter returned to Galilee to go fishing. This was another all-night fishing attempt that resulted in no fish. Zilch, zero, zippo fish.

When he was returning the next morning, a stranger on the shore called to him, "Throw your net on the right side of the boat, and you will find some fish."

Peter's mind must have flashed back three years before to the day when he made his all-time greatest catch. On that day also there was an unusual request concerning his fishing tactics, so he instinctively grabbed the nets and cast to the starboard side. The net became so full of fish that it was impossible to haul them in.

Suddenly Peter's eyes were opened and he realized that the stranger was Jesus. He threw on his coat and jumped into the water, perhaps as an act of remorse. This was the same beloved friend he had denied three nights earlier. Peter wondered, "How can I face him now?"

However, the reunion on shore was one of joy. Jesus already had prepared breakfast with grilled fish on the hot charcoal fire. After eating, Jesus said, "Follow me."

Peter's mind went back to the earlier invitation on the same Galilee docks three years before. "Well, Jesus is really saying, 'Follow me, again,'" thought Peter, "or rather, 'Keep on following me.' He is saying he still loves me, even after I have turned my back on him. He is reinstating me. I am still loved."

Peter followed Jesus again. The Book of Acts tells of his preaching, healing, and church leadership. He ultimately died a martyr's death on a cross. Tradition says that he chose to be crucified upside down, considering himself unworthy to die like his Master.

Notice the similarities of Peter's two most memorable fishing trips ever, one on the first day he met Jesus and the other on the week after Jesus' resurrection.

# TWO FISHING TRIPS
# NIGHT FISHING WITH PETER

| | Luke 5 | John 21 |
|---|---|---|
| *Initial Fishing Results:* | Fished all night, caught nothing (skunked). | Fished all night, caught nothing (skunked). |
| *Enter Jesus:* | Jesus had been teaching when he got into Peter's boat and said, "Push off shore." Then he sat down and taught from the boat. | Early in morning, Jesus stood on shore and yelled to Peter in his boat. |
| *Jesus' Command:* | "Put out into deep water and let down the nets for a catch" (result promised). | "Throw your net on the right side of boat, and you will find some" (result promised). |
| *Peter's Response:* | "Let down the nets." | Cast net on right side of boat. |
| *Final Fishing Results:* | Peter signaled another boat to help them. Both boats became so full they began to sink. (Nets broke.) | Unable to haul net in because of large number of fish (153). (Net didn't break.) |
| *Peter's Unworthiness:* | Fell at Jesus' knees and said, "Go away from me, Lord; I am a sinful man!" | Wrapped outer garment around him and jumped into water. |
| *Jesus' Invitation:* | "Don't be afraid; from now on you will catch men." | "Follow me!" (Start again—Peter was reinstated.) |
| *Peter's Response:* | Followed Jesus—left everything. | Followed Jesus—to his death. |

# Part 6

# His Final Week
## Love to Die For

# 22

# Seven Incredible Days

### Reporting Jesus' Life

The biography of Jesus Christ was written independently by four beat reporters who covered his life. These men gave us eyewitness accounts of a man they admired greatly. They wrote at different times, apparently without corroboration, each from his own perspective.

Surprisingly, none of these takes much time covering Jesus' early life (ages two to thirty); but they all give much attention to his next three years and then close with extensive reporting on his final week. That final week is the capstone of all their writings.

Take John, for example. He could have reported hundreds of miracles and dozens of sermons, yet he devoted almost half of his Gospel (ten of twenty-one chapters) to Jesus' final week.

As we have seen previously, most of Jesus' life wasn't scheduled (or at least it appeared that way). His calendar was not overbooked like a doctor's office. Instead he met people where they were. He took time to meet their needs, to answer their questions, and to teach—all without being tied to an apparent schedule. Of course, each moment of his life was ordained by God, but through our eyes it appeared random—except for his final week, that is. Then every minute was planned.

The gospel writers gave great ink to this final week. This was undoubtedly the most important week in Jesus' life, as well as the most important week in history.

# Jesus' Date Book—The Final Week

## Sunday

11:00 A.M.—Jerusalem (ride on donkey, triumphal entry parade)

## Monday

10:00 A.M.—Temple (throw out money changers)

## Tuesday

10:00 A.M.—Temple (lecture)
3:00 P.M.—Mt. of Olives (discourse)

## Wednesday

## Thursday

6:00 P.M.—Upper room (Passover Seder; last dinner with disciples)
11:00 P.M.—Garden of Gethsemane (pray)
Midnight—Betrayal (Judas) and arrest

## Friday

1:00 A.M.—Caiaphas's home (inquisition)
2:00 A.M.—Pilate's court (hearing)
3:00 A.M.—Herod's court (hearing)
4:00 A.M.—Pilate's court (rehearing)
9:00 A.M.—Mount Calvary; Golgotha—crucifixion
Noon—Darkness; earthquake
3:00 P.M.—Death

## Saturday

All day and night—Death

## Sunday

6:00 A.M.—Grave site (appear outside tomb—ALIVE)

# CHAPTERS REPORTING JESUS' LIFE

|  | Birth–30 | Last 3 Years | Final Week | Post-resurrection |
|---|---|---|---|---|
| Matthew | 1–2 (2) | 3–20 (18) | 21–28 (8) | .1 |
| Mark | none | 1–10 (10) | 11–16 (6) | .2 |
| Luke | 1–2 (2) | 3–18 (16) | 19–24 (6) | .4 |
| John | none | 1–11 (11) | 12–21 (10) | 1.2 |
|  | 4% (4) | 62% (55) | 32% (30) | 2% (1.9) |

To see this in another light, imagine that a movie is made on the life of Jesus—a three-hour epic. Instead of devoting five to six minutes to each year of Jesus' life to cover it chronologically, if we use the narratives available from our four script writers, Matthew, Mark, Luke, and John, the movie might break down like this:

# SCRIPT: THE LIFE OF JESUS

| Young Jesus | 30 Something | Final Week | Post-resurrection |
|---|---|---|---|
| Birth to 30 | 31–33 | Age 33 |  |
| 7 minutes | 1 hr. 51 mins. | 58 minutes | 4 minutes |

The first thirty years of Jesus' life in this movie take only seven minutes; the next three years take almost two hours; and the final week takes almost one-third of the movie.

So what does that tell us? The largest segment of each of the four books was during Jesus' three years of public ministry. Three years. Three short years—about a thousand days. Jesus, we hardly knew you.

And in those three short years, the entire course of history was changed—markedly, radically, eternally.

What can *you* do in a three-year period?

You could pay off a car loan, but you couldn't finish college.

You could finish law school, but you'd have no time to take the bar exam.

You could run for president, but you couldn't serve a full term.

But in Jesus' three brief years of public ministry he did far more than run for president or practice law or pay off a car loan. His mission was eternal. He was not a taker but a giver—of life, of peace, of joy far beyond man's greatest expectations.

That's why the four writers spent about two-thirds of their writing on his three public years and then zoomed in their focus on Jesus' final week—one-third of the Gospels devoted to his last seven days.

The thirty-three years of Jesus' life were only preparation for his true mission on earth—to die for sin and to destroy the power of death forever. Jesus' roles as Master Teacher and Miracle Worker were secondary to his roles as Dying Savior and Risen Lord.

---

# Death Row Watch

### Just before his death:

He led a parade.
He routed the money changers.
He taught about love.
He hosted a dinner.
He took communion.
He washed dirty feet.
He answered trite questions.
He prayed alone.
He comforted others.
He healed an ear.
He forgave his assassins.

### His death prompted:

One convict release
Two other crucifixions
One suicide
One angel appearance
Soldiers out cold
Two bribes
Lies and cover-ups
Two earthquakes
One solar eclipse
Appearances of resurrected saints
One lasting resurrection
Salvation

# 23

# Jesus, Meet
# the Press

Emerson wrote, "He who has a thousand friends has not a friend to spare; And he who has one enemy will meet him everywhere."

An enemy, according to Webster, is "one that is antagonistic to another." If that's so, Jesus certainly had a few and they were a busy bunch as they followed him around, seeking to harm him.

Ever wonder why the kind, compassionate, and caring Jesus would have any enemies? After all, who could dislike anyone who healed the sick and taught about love? What drove Jesus' enemies to hate?

That's what makes the words of the Pharisees, key players on Team Enemy, worthy of study. Let's eavesdrop on their board meetings and see what ticked them off.

**How to Think Like a Hypocrite**

Jesus spent much of his recorded addresses talking to and about the Pharisees. Why? Perhaps it's because their words sounded holy but their actions were otherwise. Or perhaps it's because they were misusing their religious authority for other purposes, such as political or financial advantage.

Whatever the case, the Pharisees were very high on Jesus' list, and Jesus was very high on the Pharisees' list. This foreign object had appeared on the Pharisees' radar screen, and he was a threat to the very authority of their office. So they responded, in three different ways—

they plotted against him, they asked him trick questions, and they tried character assassination.

### 1. Boardroom Plots: Strategy Sessions

The first stage was the scheming stage, discussing how they might trap Jesus. Listen in on some of the Pharisees' actual comments and sense their confusion and frustration.

"How can he know so much when he's never been to our schools?" (John 7:15).

"Where is he planning to go? Maybe he is thinking of leaving the country and going as a missionary among the Jews in other lands, or maybe even to the Gentiles! What does he mean about our looking for him and not being able to find him, and 'You won't be able to come where I am'?" (John 7:35–36).

"Is he planning suicide? What does he mean, 'You cannot come where I am going'?" (John 8:22).

"What are we going to do? For this man certainly does miracles. If we let him alone the whole nation will follow him—and then the Roman army will come and kill us and take over the Jewish government" (John 11:47–48).

"We've lost. Look—the whole world has gone after him!" (John 12:19).

### 2. Tricks, Traps, and Taunts: Jesus, Meet the Press

After scheming in the boardroom came the questioning phase. Try to trap Jesus. Ask him all of those trick questions that had been carefully conceived in closed-door sessions. Put him on the spot. Jesus, meet the press.

Luke writes, "The Pharisees and legal experts were furious; and from that time on they plied him fiercely with a host of questions, trying to trap him into saying something for which they could have him arrested" (Luke 11:53–54).

It was only natural that the Pharisees would try to trap Jesus with trick questions. After all, who knew more about the law than this esteemed religious body? And besides, their word was final, not subject to appeal. This is one game they couldn't lose.

I would love to have listened in when the Pharisees heard from Judge Gamaliel, chairman of the How to Deal with Jesus Committee.

# MINUTES OF THE REGULAR MEETING OF PHARISEES AND CO.
## JUNE 7

The regular monthly meeting of the Pharisees was held on Tuesday, June 7th, at the home of Simeon, at 6:00 P.M. All were present except Nicodemus, who had another appointment he couldn't cancel.

*Call to Order.* Chairman Nathan called the meeting to order and thanked Mrs. Simeon for the bagels and coffee.

*Minutes of Previous Meeting.* The reading of the minutes of the May meeting was waived.

*Treasurer's Report.* The treasurer Hosea reported that offerings for May were down 16%, a grave cause for concern.

### Old Business

1. *Justice System Review.* Chief Priest Caiaphas reported on his investigation in the Jerusalem courts. The judges are overworked, calendars are full, and the local justice system is in gridlock.

The prisons are also filled to capacity. In a recent tour of the prisons, he noted that in one tiny cell built for a single prisoner, three prisoners were crammed inside—Barabbas, the violent serial killer, with two eighteen-year-olds who appeared terrified.

These jail conditions are inhumane and must be rectified. More prisons may not be the answer. Caiaphas recommends releasing some of the less violent prisoners, perhaps starting with first-timers, or "white-collar" inmates.

2. *New Stained Glass Windows.* In view of the present financial decline, the new windows request was tabled.

### New Business

*Complaints against Jesus of Nazareth.* Caiaphas reported that he had received a large number of complaints about Jesus, the recent high-profile visitor to Jerusalem. Even synagogue meetings have been disturbed. Rabbi Caleb told how he had been speaking last week when there were loud cheers in the street, so the people inside ran out to see what had happened. Supposedly, Jesus had healed Abe, the blind man, and the crowd went crazy. The people never returned for the rest of the lesson.

A lengthy discussion over this problem then ensued. Many suggestions were offered during an emotional and oft confusing exchange. Due to the lateness of the meeting, the chairman then appointed a How to Deal with Jesus Committee to be chaired by learned Judge Gamaliel, who will report back at the July meeting.

There being no further business, the lights were finally blown out at 11:30 P.M.

Respectfully submitted,

*Micah*

Micah, Secretary

# M E M O

## CONFIDENTIAL REPORT

### How to Deal with Jesus

To:    Chief Priest Caiaphas
From: Judge Gamaliel, Chairman
      How to Deal with Jesus Committee

At our June meeting, I was asked to chair this new committee. Little did I realize how timely this would become, especially in light of Jesus' violent overthrow of the temple money changers last Friday.

Our committee has been busy interviewing followers of Jesus, including some allegedly "healed" former hospital patients. We have also tracked Jesus for a full week, sitting in on eight major addresses and two dozen mini-sessions.

This Jesus has a most charismatic personality. He's a natural salesman—just so happens he's selling religion. His sermons are simplistic and childlike.

Recommendation: I think we can stop this Jesus fad by letting him trip himself up. He's never been to our seminary. Let's ask him some tough theological questions in front of a crowd. He'll be surprised and embarrassed and speechless. Then we'll turn to the crowd and take over; remind them about our upcoming meetings. Simple.

I recommend asking him questions like, "Who gave you the authority to walk in here and pop off? Why are your followers not keeping our laws? What's the most important command?"

After facing a few of these, he'll wish he'd never tangled with us, I can assure you.

Here are some of the actual questions the Pharisees presented to embarrass Jesus in public meetings.

"Is it legal to work by healing on the Sabbath day?" (Matt. 12:10).
"Do you permit divorce?" (Matt. 19:3).
"Why did Moses say a man may divorce his wife by merely writing her a letter of dismissal?" (Matt. 19:7).
"Why don't your disciples follow our age-old customs? For they eat without first performing the washing ceremony" (Mark 7:5).

"[Your disciples are feasting instead of fasting.] John the Baptist's disciples are constantly going without food, and praying, and so do the disciples of the Pharisees. Why are yours wining and dining?" (Luke 5:33).

"Your disciples are breaking the law. They are harvesting on the Sabbath" (Matt. 12:2).

"Who gave you the authority to drive out the [temple] merchants?" (Mark 11:28).

"Which is the most important command in the laws of Moses?" (Matt. 22:36).

"Teacher, we know you tell the truth, no matter what! You aren't influenced by the opinions and desires of men, but sincerely teach the ways of God. Now tell us, is it right to pay taxes to Rome, or not?" (Mark 12:14).

"What we want to know is this: In the resurrection, whose wife will she be, for she had been the wife of each of them?" (Mark 12:23).

"Which neighbors [must I love]?" (Luke 10:29).

"If you aren't the Messiah or Elijah or the Prophet, what right do you have to baptize?" (John 1:24–25).

"What right have you to order them [the money changers] out? If you have this authority from God, show us a miracle to prove it" (John 2:18).

"What! It took forty-six years to build this Temple, and you can do it in three days?" (John 2:20).

"Teacher, this woman was caught in the very act of adultery. Moses' law says to kill her. What about it?" (John 8:4–5).

"We have never been slaves to any man on earth! What do you mean [the truth shall] 'set [us] free'?" (John 8:33).

"How long are you going to keep us in suspense? If you are the Messiah, tell us plainly" (John 10:24).

### 3. Winning through Intimidation: Power from Position

Once the Pharisees found that their trick questions didn't stump Jesus, they then attacked his character, calling him names, insulting him, and ridiculing him. In the courtroom, if you don't have a good defense, attack the witness's character. If you can't win an argument rationally, attack the person. Taken to its extreme, it becomes character assassination.

# M E M O

## C O N F I D E N T I A L   R E P O R T   # 2

**How to Deal with Jesus**

To: Caiaphas, High Priest
From: Judge Gamaliel, Chairman
      How to Deal with Jesus Committee

Well, our "Trick Jesus and Let Him Fall on His Face" game plan hasn't worked. Never did I think he could handle all the questions we threw at him. Some were questions our own Ph.D.'s couldn't answer. And worse yet, he really embarrassed us in the process. According to the latest JNN poll, our popularity is dropping like a watermelon off the city walls. The crowds following him are continuing to grow. People are coming from miles around to hear him—especially sick people. Problem is, they don't stay sick!

But how does he do it? That's what our committee has been considering. How can he know so much? How can he do these miracles? How can he cast out demons?

We figured out how to handle it. Let's say he's got one himself. Only a demon could order another demon around. Yep, takes one to know one. And that would explain why he hangs around with such riffraff.

Recommendation: Let's expose Jesus for what he is—a demon-possessed fraud, who's leading our people astray. Let's circulate handbills, leak stories about the demon connection, knock his disciples, whatever it takes.

When the Pharisees' attempts to trick Jesus had failed, their plan exploded in their faces; they were the ones embarrassed when Jesus answered every question.

Watch how this not-so-subtle character assassination was aimed at Jesus and his followers through actual quotes of the Pharisees.

> "The reason he can cast out demons is that he is demon-possessed himself—possessed by Satan, the demon king!" (Matt. 9:34).
> "What? This is blasphemy! Does he think he is God? For only God can forgive sins" (Mark 2:7).

"This proves that Jesus is no prophet, for if God had really sent him, he would know what kind of woman this one is!" (Luke 7:39).

"Who does this man think he is, going around forgiving sins?" (Luke 7:49).

"You are boasting—and lying!" (John 8:13).

"You Samaritan! Foreigner! Devil! Didn't we say all along you were possessed by a demon?" (John 8:48).

"Give the glory to God, not to Jesus, for we know Jesus is an evil person" (John 9:24).

"He has a demon or else is crazy. Why listen to a man like that?" (John 10:20).

"Now we know you are possessed by a demon. Even Abraham and the mightiest prophets died, and yet you say that obeying you will keep a man from dying! So you are greater than our father Abraham, who died? Who do you think you are?" (John 8:52–53).

### Enemies: A Love Story

Because of their opposition to Jesus, we often think of the Pharisees as dirty rotten scoundrels. But the fact is that they were considered good people. Very good people. Many of them were sincerely trying to live impeccably pure lives. That's why they added all their extra laws—so that people wouldn't break God's laws even by accident. If the nation was righteous enough, they figured, God would send the Messiah, who would then free them from those nasty Romans.

Isn't it ironic that these "good" people (or at least some of them) would miss the Messiah when he came?

Then there were the Romans, who had a strong sense of nobility and morality. Order was all-important. Good citizenship meant good behavior.

But when a folk hero named Jesus began to disrupt things, he had to be stopped. By crucifixion if need be.

These were the players on Team Enemy. Not the snarling, spitting bad guys we might expect, but good, upstanding citizens—respected leaders in the community. If I lived in those days, I would be proud to be a Pharisee, a scribe, or a Roman lawyer. They stood for the things I stand for—righteousness, truth, and justice.

What happened? Pride crept in. Greed. Power hunger. Like a snake slithering up a tree, self-interest took hold of these well-meaning leaders. It's been the same story since the Garden of Eden: Good things can turn bad in one bite.

It's interesting that the early believers—Team Disciples—didn't spend a whole lot of time trying to fix the blame for Jesus' death. Peter, preaching within two months after the crucifixion, told a crowd of thousands about Jesus, whom "you crucified." He also said, "God, following his prearranged plan, let you use the Roman government to nail him to the cross and murder him" (Acts 2:23, 36).

What's this "prearranged plan" all about? It goes back to Eden and Jesus' whole mission statement. The taste of that forbidden fruit began the decay of God's A+ creation. Sin spread to all humanity and created a need for redemption.

It was sin that put Jesus on the cross. Whether we look at the power lust of Caiaphas or the cowardice of Pilate or the greed of Judas or our own sins, we are all on Team Enemy.

Paul told the Roman church, "God showed his great love for us by sending Christ to die for us while we were still sinners" (Rom. 5:8). Jesus' death was God's way of making us friends again.

# 24

# Night Court

How can a judge rig a trial to convict an innocent man? How do you turn a friendly crowd into a frenzied mob? How do you legitimize the execution of the Son of God?

Just watch—through the eyes and actions of the presiding judge.

Jesus' trial before Pilate began with an emergency call to the Governor's Mansion in the middle of the night. An angry mob was chanting outside, and a bloodied and battered Jesus was pushed along before Pilate. There a dazed governor took jurisdiction over history's most unforgettable trial.

All of these court proceedings were heard within hours of each other by a governor/acting judge who had undoubtedly gone without sleep most of the night.

I have carefully tried to correlate Jesus' trial before Pilate into chronological sequence, using actual quotes of the parties involved as much as possible. The proceedings were then typed as a transcript, as if prepared by a court reporter.

I presented this transcript to two federal judges, William Hoeveler and Peter Fay. Their critique of Pilate's handling of Jesus' trial was indeed enlightening. What follows, therefore, is Jesus' trial transcript with most of the marginal comments by Judges Hoeveler and Fay. The final result according to Judge Fay was a "complete subversion of the Roman judicial system, which was at that time a sophisticated justice system."

All rise. Court is in session. The Honorable Justice Pontius Pilate presiding.

Try to read between the lines into Pilate's very soul. Is this a mighty leader of the people or a wimpy bureaucrat anxious to satisfy a bloodthirsty crowd? Is it Jesus who is on trial, or is it Judge Pilate himself?[1]

---

## ROMAN EMPIRE

v.

## JESUS CHRIST

IN THE ROMAN COURT
IN JERUSALEM
CRIMINAL DIVISION

File Number: LVI
Division: viii

Judge: PONTIUS PILATE

*Transcript of pre-trial hearings. NO trial ever held.*

TRANSCRIPT OF TRIAL

*Presumption of defendant's guilt, not innocence.*

ARRAIGNMENT—EARLY A.M. Defendant Jesus in chains.

PILATE: "What is your charge against this man? What are you accusing him of doing?"

*Ruling #1— Order denying Roman jurisdiction.*

CHIEF PRIESTS AND JEWISH LEADERS: "We wouldn't have arrested him if he wasn't a criminal!"

PILATE: "Then take him away and judge him yourselves by your own laws."

*Capital punishment required Roman order.*

CHIEF PRIESTS: "But we want him crucified, and your approval is required."

PILATE: Went back to palace, then called for defendant Jesus to be brought before him.

*Ruling #2— Order accepting Roman jurisdiction, reversing Ruling #1.*

CHIEF PRIESTS AND JEWISH LEADERS: "This fellow has been leading our people to ruin by telling them not to pay their taxes to the Roman Government and by claiming he is our Messiah—a King."

PILATE: "Are you the Jews' Messiah? The King of the Jews?"

DEFENDANT JESUS: "'King' as you use the word, or as the Jews use it?"

*Criminal charge— tax evasion? sedition? Are these capital crimes?*

PILATE: "Am I a Jew? Your own people and their Chief Priests brought you here. Why? What have you done?"

*Jesus not represented by counsel.*

DEFENDANT JESUS: "I am not an earthly king. If I were, my followers would have fought when I was arrested by the Jewish leaders. But my kingdom is not of this world."

PILATE: "But are you a king then?"

DEFENDANT JESUS: "Yes, I was born for that purpose. And I came to bring truth to the world. All who love truth are my followers."

PILATE: "What is truth?" (To the crowd) "He is not guilty of any crime."

CHIEF PRIESTS: "But he claims to be king."

PILATE: "So? That isn't a crime!"

(Chief Priests and crowd became desperate and accused him of many other crimes. Defendant Jesus stood silent.)

PILATE: "Don't you hear what they're saying? Why don't you say something? What about all these charges against you?"

(Defendant Jesus stood silent.)

CHIEF PRIESTS: "He is causing riots against the governor everywhere he goes, all over Judea, from Galilee to Jerusalem."

PILATE: "Is he then a Galilean? Take him to King Herod, for Herod has jurisdiction over Galilee."

(Note: After accusations, shouting, and mocking, Herod found him innocent and sent Defendant Jesus back to Pilate. "That day Herod and Pilate—enemies before—became fast friends" [Luke 23:12].)

LATER IN MORNING.

PILATE'S WIFE SENT MESSENGER TO PILATE: "Leave that good man alone; for I had a terrible nightmare concerning him last night."

PILATE: "You brought this man to me, accusing him of leading a revolt against the Roman government. I have examined him thoroughly on this point and find him innocent. Herod came to the same conclusion and sent him back to us—nothing this man has done calls for the death penalty. I will therefore have him punished and release him."

PILATE (continued): "But you have a custom of asking me to release someone from prison each year at Passover. So, if you want me to, I'll release the King of the Jews. Which shall I release to you—Barabbas (convicted murderer) or Jesus, your Messiah?"

("For he realized by now that this was a frame-up, backed by the chief priests because they envied Jesus' popularity" Mark 15:10.)

CHIEF PRIESTS: Whipped up the mob to demand the release of Barabbas instead of Jesus.

PILATE: "But if I release Barabbas, what shall I do with Jesus, your Messiah—this man you call your king?"

---

*Margin annotations (handwritten):*

Ruling #3— Pilate issues order "not guilty of any crime." i.e., no probable cause, defendant should be released.

Jesus had no right to remain silent like 5th Amendment in US today.

New charges made.

Ruling #4— Pilate again accepts jurisdiction.

Ruling #5— Pilate issues order transferring Jesus to Herod. Herod acquits Jesus, yet retains jurisdiction to send case back to Pilate.

Ruling #6— Pilate finds Jesus "innocent" of inciting riots. Another dismissal of charges.

Ruling #7— Pilate issues order punishing defendant—"Teach him a lesson!" But why the continued jurisdiction after charges dropped? Unexplained bargaining with crowd.

Ruling #8— Pilate issues yet another order dismissing charges and releasing defendant.

Ruling #9— Pilate reassumes jurisdiction after prior rulings had released Jesus. Then Pilate attempts compromise with the crowd, seeks their opinion on the issue before the court.

Ruling #10—Pilate issued yet another order dismissing charges; acquittal.

Ruling #11—Pilate issued order of scourging.

Ruling #12—yet another release order. Pilate's self-declaration of innocence, Then shifts blame to crowd.

Jesus probably received 39 lashes with leaded whip ("Cruel and unusual punishment" under US law—8th Am.). After Jesus had received favorable due process.

Ruling #13—Order of Acquittal after Jesus just released.

"Power" perhaps, but not the "courage" to release Jesus.

Ruling #14—Pilate issues one more release order.

Pilate now warned. Any appeals from his court go to Caesar.

Pilate plays with the crowd.

Ruling #15—Pilate issues order of execution by crucifixion even though no valid charges, no trial, no finding of guilt, no right of appeal.

Ruling #16—Order releasing Barabbas.

Ruling #17—Order releasing Jesus to lynch mob—"Do as you wish."

MOB: "Crucify him. Crucify him."

PILATE: (For third time) "Why? What crime has he committed? I have found no reason to sentence him to death. I will therefore scourge him and let him go."

PILATE: Laid open Jesus' back with the leaded whip.

SOLDIERS: Made a crown of thorns and placed it on his head and robed him in royal purple. "Hail, King of the Jews." They mocked him and struck him with their fists.

PILATE: "I am going to bring him out to you now, but understand clearly that I find him not guilty."

JESUS: Came out wearing crown of thorns and purple robe.

PILATE: "You won't talk to me. Don't you realize that I have the power to release you or to crucify you?"

JESUS: "You would have no power at all over me unless it were given you from others. So those who brought me to you have the greater sin."

PILATE: "I will release this man."

CROWD: "If you release this man you are no friend of Caesar's. Anyone who declares himself a king is a rebel against Caesar."

PILATE: Brought Jesus out to them again and sat down at the judgment bench. "Here is your king."

CROWD: "Away with him. Away with him. Crucify him."

PILATE: "What? Crucify your king?"

CHIEF PRIESTS: "We have no king but Caesar."

PILATE: Seeing that he wasn't getting anywhere, and that a riot was developing, he was (1) afraid of a riot and (2) anxious to please the people (Mark 15:15).

MOB: Shouted louder and louder for Jesus' death, "and their voices prevailed" (Luke 23:23).

PILATE: Sent for bowl of water and washed his hands before crowd. "I am innocent of the blood of this good man. The responsibility is yours."

MOB: "His blood be on us and our children."

PILATE: Sentenced Jesus to death as they demanded, "Crucify him." Released Barabbas at their request. "Here is Barabbas." Delivered Jesus over to them to do with as they would. "Here is Jesus. Do with him as you please."

# ADMINISTRATIVE ORDERS

## 1. RE: SHALL THE SIGN ON THE CROSS BE CHANGED?

*Ruling #18—Pilate issues order posting sign on cross.*

PILATE: "Post a sign on the cross above his head: 'Jesus of Nazareth, King of the Jews.'"

CHIEF PRIESTS: "Change it from 'The King of the Jews' to 'He said, I am King of the Jews.'"

*Ruling #19—Petition to modify sign denied. (Pilate suddenly has a backbone!)*

PILATE: "What I have written I have written. It stays exactly as it is."

## 2. RE: SHALL JESUS' BODY BE GIVEN TO JOSEPH OF ARIMATHEA?

PILATE: "Is Jesus dead?"

ROMAN OFFICER: "Yes."

*Ruling #20—Pilate issued order releasing Jesus' corpse for burial.*

PILATE: Issued order to release Jesus' body to Joseph of Arimathea and handed it to him saying, "Here is the order to release Jesus' body to you" (Matt. 27:57–58).

## 3. RE: SHALL THE TOMB BE SEALED?

The next day was the close of the first day of Passover.

CHIEF PRIESTS: "Sir, that liar once said, 'After three days I will come back to life again.' So, we request an order from you sealing the tomb until the third day to prevent his disciples from coming and stealing his body and then telling everyone he came back to life! If that happens we'll be worse off than we were at first!"

*Ruling #21—Order denying request to guard and seal tomb.*

PILATE: "Use your own temple police. They can guard it safely enough."

Twenty-one rulings and three dead men later, Judge Pilate went back to the palace to sleep (or try to).

[1]Special thanks to Senior U.S. District Judge William Hoeveler (Southern District, Florida), who incidentally presided in the landmark case against Panamanian President Manuel Noriega, and Senior U.S. Judge Peter Fay (11th Circuit Court of Appeals), for their narrative comments on Judge Pilate's day on the bench.

# 25

# His Final Day

The earthly end had come for Jesus. His final day had arrived. After thirty-three years in human form, this would be his final day on Planet Earth—day number 12,045. He would soon go home to his father.

Just as Jesus' first-time events were memorable, so would be his final events—his final meal, his final anointing, and his final good-byes.

How were his final twenty-four hours spent? As best we know, these memorable moments on Thursday and Friday looked something like the chart on the next page.

As I read over this list of individuals who played a part in Jesus' final day (whether a major or minor part), I notice a few things.

First of all, most of the people listed were either pro-Jesus or anti-Jesus. By now their allegiance was established, even though some weren't willing to admit it at times, like Peter. Read the list and see how easy it is to identify the loyalties of each.

Second, notice the weapons collection; weapons to torture and kill—swords, clubs, spears, crown of thorns, wine/gall, wine vinegar, sponge, hammer, nails, and crosses. I wonder who was in charge of the equipment room.

And third, of all the incidents covered by the gospel writers, only nine events were covered by all four.

1. Jesus' preaching in Galilee
2. Jesus' feeding the 5,000
3. Jesus' riding a donkey into Jerusalem
4. The Last Supper

# THE FINAL TWENTY-FOUR HOURS
# DAY NO. 12,045

| | Time | Event | People | Props |
|---|---|---|---|---|
| **THURSDAY** | 7:00–10:00 P.M. | Passover | Jesus<br>Disciples | Table<br>Passover meal<br>Cup<br>Wine<br>Bread<br>Water bowl<br>Towel |
| | 10:00 P.M.–<br>midnight | Garden Arrest | Jesus<br>Disciples<br>Pharisees<br>Officials<br>High Priest<br>Malchus, servant<br>Angel<br>Judas<br>Young man<br>Soldiers | Swords<br>Clubs<br>Disciples' swords (2)<br>Ear (severed)<br>Linen garment<br>30 pieces of silver<br>Rope (noose) |
| **FRIDAY** | Midnight–<br>6:00 A.M. | Denial | Jesus<br>Peter<br>Servant girls<br>Malchus's relative | Logs<br>Fire<br>Rooster |
| | Midnight–<br>7:30 A.M. | Trials | Jesus<br>Annas<br>False witnesses<br>Sanhedrin<br>Crowd<br>Caiaphas<br>Barabbas<br>Pilate<br>Pilate's wife | Judge's seat<br>Purple robe<br>Water bowl<br>Towel<br>Crown of thorns<br>Whips<br>Blindfold<br>Staff |
| | 9:00 A.M.–<br>3:00 P.M. | Crucifixion | Jesus<br>Two thieves<br>Gawkers<br>Simon<br>Mary<br>Mother's sister<br>Mary, wife of Clophas<br>Mary Magdalene<br>John | Three crosses<br>Nails<br>Hammer<br>Jesus' robe<br>Dice<br>Wine/gall<br>Wine vinegar<br>Sponge<br>Stalk of hyssop plant<br>Spear<br>Swords |
| | 3:00–<br>6:00 P.M. | Burial | Jesus<br>Joseph of Arimathea<br>Nicodemus | Clean linen<br>Myrrh<br>Aloes |

5. Peter's denial of Jesus
6. Jesus' trial and sentencing by Pilate
7. The crucifixion
8. Jesus' burial
9. Jesus' resurrection

The special significance of these nine events is obvious because of the four-network coverage. Jesus' preaching in Galilee and feeding of 5,000 occurred during his public ministry (Thirtysomething). The other seven events occurred in his final week. And that's the end of the story—or rather, the beginning!

### Special Awards

I would like to make some posthumous awards to certain individuals whom I feel deserve special recognition.

*Best of Both Worlds (NOT!) Award*—to Judas Iscariot. Judas wanted it all, the best of both worlds. He wanted to be on the inner circle of both Jesus and the Pharisees and to make money off both of them in the process. For one brief moment, he thought he had it made, but the price was too great. He died hours later, penniless, a suicide.

*Bad News/Good News Award*—to Malchus. This young servant of the high priest stayed late for work one night. But this was not his usual overtime assignment. He accompanied the high priest to the garden where he witnessed firsthand Jesus' arrest. Unfortunately he was standing next to the high priest when Peter showed off his lightning-fast sword maneuver. Malchus never saw it coming—never even had a chance to duck. Malchus lost an ear, but he got a new one a few moments later when the Master Physician performed his final healing. For Malchus, it was one of those bad news/good news days he'd never forget!

*Rambo/Chicken Award*—to Simon Peter. The Ever-Present-in-Time-of-Danger Peter was trigger-happy when Jesus was arrested. He even brought along two swords for the occasion, and he used one quite effectively. I don't know who he was aiming at—the high priest or the servant—or what he was aiming at—the head or ear—but he severed one ear very cleanly. After brandishing a weapon in a crowd of enemy soldiers, is it any wonder that Peter went undercover for the rest of the night? In fact, within hours the same loyal defender was denying his about-to-be-slain leader.

*Woman's Intuition Award*—to Pilate's wife, Mrs. Pilate. We don't know much about her except:

1.  She was interested in seeing justice served (more so than her husband/governor/judge).
2.  She wasn't afraid to advise her husband/governor/judge.
3.  She warned her husband to let Jesus go—she knew he was innocent.

Imagine the breakfast table conversation on Easter morning at the Governor's Mansion just as Pilate got word that Jesus was alive and appearing all over Jerusalem. Do you think he might have heard "I told you so!" at least once while the toast was burning?

*Wash All My Troubles Away Award*—to Pilate. Pilate, never try a capital case with your political hat on. You weren't chairing a floor debate on a bill, you were deciding whether a man lived or died. You should have listened to your wife! After sentencing Jesus to death, Pilate tried to convince his constituents (and himself) that he had played no part in the proceedings by publicly washing his hands. It is curious that in Jesus' final twenty-four hours, two different water bowls are described. One was used by Jesus at the Last Supper, and the other was used by Pilate. One was used to wash feet as the final act of a servant, and the other was used to wash hands in an attempt to cleanse guilt.

*Mr. Lucky Award*—to Barabbas. Convicted felon Barabbas was on death row, awaiting his execution, when he got the unexpected announcement, "You're free; go on home. Jesus is taking your place!" Barabbas had indeed dodged a bullet—the big one! It was his lucky day!

*God's Grace Award*—to the unnamed thief who died alongside Jesus and believed on him in his final moments of life. As his life was ebbing away, he called out to Jesus (only inches away), who responded to his plea, "Today, you will be with me in Paradise." Just imagine. Here was a career criminal, while being executed for a capital crime, becoming a believer for perhaps ten minutes and then entering into paradise, side by side with the Son of God! This was not because of Mr. Thief's good luck, and certainly not because of his good works or rehabilitated condition, but solely by the grace of God.

# Two Thieves

*Conversation at the Cross*

(Luke 23:34–46)

During his final moments of agony on a cross, Jesus was placed between two thieves. Two men would die deaths they deserved; the other would die a death that mankind deserved.

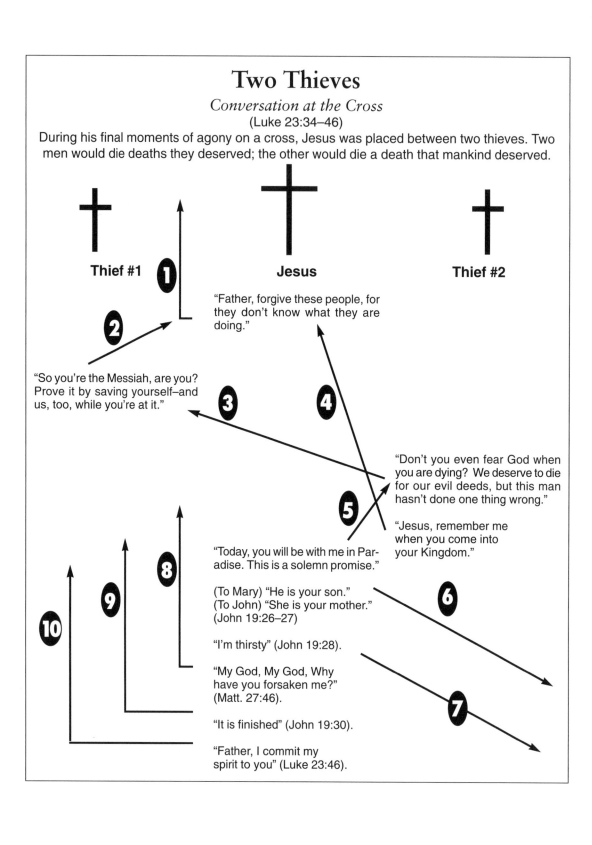

**Thief #1**

**Jesus**

**Thief #2**

"Father, forgive these people, for they don't know what they are doing."

"So you're the Messiah, are you? Prove it by saving yourself–and us, too, while you're at it."

"Don't you even fear God when you are dying? We deserve to die for our evil deeds, but this man hasn't done one thing wrong."

"Jesus, remember me when you come into your Kingdom."

"Today, you will be with me in Paradise. This is a solemn promise."

(To Mary) "He is your son."
(To John) "She is your mother."
(John 19:26–27)

"I'm thirsty" (John 19:28).

"My God, My God, Why have you forsaken me?" (Matt. 27:46).

"It is finished" (John 19:30).

"Father, I commit my spirit to you" (Luke 23:46).

# Part 7

# Alive and Well

## The Forever Family

# 26

# Estate Planning

### Last Wills of the Rich and Famous

My law practice is largely estate planning, so I have a natural fascination for wills. I am fascinated by the way people leave their earthly belongings.

Elizabeth Richey had a burden for the homeless—homeless dogs, that is. She kept 150 dogs at her Ft. Lauderdale farm until she died. In her will, she left her dogs to Auburn University, together with $2.5 million to take care of them. That works out to about $17,000 a mutt, which should keep them in Alpo for a while.

Pablo Picasso refused to make a will, thinking that was the best way of avoiding death. He died intestate.

Elizabeth Arden left an estate of $50 million. Of this amount, she left $11 million to family, maids, servants, and 200 employees. The other $39 million went to New York State and the IRS—involuntarily, of course.

In his will, King Henry VIII provided that he be buried next to Jane, the favorite of his six wives.

William Shakespeare left everything to his two daughters and omitted his wife, except for "my 2nd best bed with the furniture."

In his will, George Washington granted freedom to his mulatto slave, William Lee. Lee then became famous and, following his death, was "buried" five times—in North Carolina, Arkansas, Missouri, and twice in New York.

Socialist Karl Marx accumulated no personal wealth, leaving only 250 pounds.

Margaret Nothe left her will written on the page of her hand-written book of kitchen recipes entitled *Chili Sauce without Working:*

4 quarts of ripe tomatoes, 4 small onions, 4 green peppers, 2 teacups of sugar, 2 quarts of cider vinegar, 2 ounces ground allspice, 2 ounces cloves, 2 ounces cinnamon, 12 teaspoons salt. Chop tomatoes, onions and peppers fine, add the rest mixed together and bottle cold. Measure tomatoes when peeled. In case I die before my husband I leave everything to him.

Adolf Hitler's will mentioned that he and Eva Braun were marrying and then choosing to die to "escape the shame of overthrow or capitulation."

Marilyn Monroe bequeathed over $1 million, but it was never paid. Her estate was declared insolvent because of large debts.

Bobby Kennedy named his brother John as executor of his will. However, John had been assassinated four years earlier, and Bobby, the former attorney general, had failed to change his own will.

The father of the late Grace Kelly, John Kelly Sr., wrote his will in layman's language. He wrote:

This is my last will, and I believe I am of sound mind. (Some lawyers may question this when they read my will, however, I have my opinion of some of them, so that makes it even.) I can think of nothing more ghastly than heirs sitting around listening to some representative reading a will. They always remind me of buzzards and vultures, awaiting the last breath of the stricken. . . . I have written this will in a lighter vein because I have always felt that wills were so dreary that they might have been written by the author of "Inner Sanctum" . . . If I don't stop soon, this will be as long as "Gone with the Wind," so just remember, when I shove off for greener pastures or whatever is on the other side of the curtain, that I do it unafraid and if you must know, a little curious.

The shortest known will in the United States was written by a lady in Queens, New York, who died in 1972. Her will provided: "Dearest George. All I have is what you gave me, so everything I have is yours. Lovingly, Helen."

Possibly the wealthiest man of all time was King Solomon. When he was preparing his will, he said:

I am disgusted about this, that I must leave the fruits of all my hard work to others. And who can tell whether my son will be a wise man or a fool?

And yet all I have will be given to him—how discouraging! . . . I must leave all of it to someone who hasn't done a day's work in his life; he inherits all my efforts, free of charge. This is not only foolish, but unfair.

Ecclesiastes 2:18–22

Dr. Patrick Henry wrote in his will:

I have now disposed of all my property to my family. There is one thing more I wish I could give them, and that is faith in Jesus Christ. If they had that, and I had not given them one shilling, they would be rich. And if I had not given them that, and I had given them all the world, they would be poor, indeed.

And speaking of Jesus Christ, I have found that his will was the most interesting one of all.

**The Will of Jesus Christ**

Jesus left a nuncupative will—a rare breed among wills because it is an oral will that is used only in limited cases. A nuncupative will is recognized in certain jurisdictions when an individual is facing imminent death and speaks his testamentary intention to a witness, who in turn transcribes what was said as soon as possible afterward. For example, if a soldier shot in combat gives dying instructions to his foxhole partner, those oral instructions may be upheld as a nuncupative will.

The same is true of deathbed instructions given to a doctor shortly before a patient dies. These wishes can later be legally formalized as a will when the doctor records his patient's spoken words.

Did Jesus Christ, by his words to his disciples, leave a nuncupative will? Let's see whether the requisite elements were present.

1. *Testator's Awareness of His Own Imminent Death.* On the night before his death, was Jesus Christ fully aware that his time had come?

- He prayed, "Now my heart is troubled, and what shall I say? 'Father, save me from this hour'? No, it was for this very reason I came to this hour" (John 12:27 NIV).
- He said, "But I, when I am lifted up from the earth, will draw all men to myself." He said this to show the kind of death he was going to die (John 12:32–33 NIV).
- He said, "In a little while you will see me no more" (John 16:19 NIV).

- He told his disciples, "The hour has come for the Son of Man to be glorified" (John 12:23 NIV).

On the night before his death, Jesus knew that his death sentence was ready to be executed. He was on death row, preparing to face the end. At his final meal, he was the waiter. There would be no attempt to escape.

*2. Testator's Oral Testament.* On the night before his death, did Jesus Christ speak words conveying testamentary meaning and intent?

In the final hours of Jesus' life, at his last meal and during prayer time in the garden, he gave specific instructions and bequests, such as, "My peace I give you [my disciples]" (John 14:27 NIV). Jesus spoke words of testamentary intent.

*3. Testator's Sound Mind.* On the night before his death, was Jesus Christ of sound mind?

There is nothing to suggest that he was not of sound mind. He even refused to take a sedative to dull the pain while on the cross the next day (Matt. 27:34).

*4. Testator's Words Transcribed.* Following the death of Jesus, were his words subsequently transcribed?

Yes, not just by one, but by four of his disciples—Matthew, Mark, Luke, and John.

*5. Testator's Legal Domicile.* Under the laws of Israel, Jesus' earthly domicile, were nuncupative wills recognized?

Although the ancient probate laws governing wills in Israel are not available for study, the present-day laws of Israel recognize a verbal nuncupative will if it is recorded by at least two witnesses. This condition was satisfied by twice the required number of witnesses.

If the four gospel writers had come to my office today to prepare Jesus' verbal will, the following is how I would have prepared the legal document.

I have attempted to prepare his will in a manner that I trust captures his final wishes and brings no discredit to or does not detract from his actual words. Much of this will is taken from John chapters 13–17, which cover Jesus' last hours before death.

In view of the foregoing, I present my personal interpretation of the nuncupative Last Will and Testament of Jesus Christ, verbally delivered within hours of his imminent death and recorded by four separate witnesses, now presented in the language of the twentieth century.

# 𝕷𝖆𝖘𝖙 𝖂𝖎𝖑𝖑 𝖆𝖓𝖉 𝕿𝖊𝖘𝖙𝖆𝖒𝖊𝖓𝖙

of

JESUS CHRIST

(Nuncupative Will)

I, JESUS CHRIST, do hereby make, publish, and declare this to be my Last Will and Testament, my lasting covenant.

ARTICLE I.

DECLARATION OF DOMICILE

Having been born in a Bethlehem barn with no known address, having then moved to Egypt for two years to no known address, having then moved to Nazareth for my childhood years, having then moved to Capernaum until evicted, I have no earthly place to call my home, but I claim a dual citizenship somewhere in Israel and in the Kingdom of God. I am fully aware that I will face my death tomorrow by crucifixion, at which time I will depart my Israel domicile and return to the Kingdom of God from whence I came.

ARTICLE II.

NOMINATION OF EXECUTOR

A. I hereby nominate and appoint the Everlasting Father, God Almighty, the Creator, as executor of my Last Will and Testament. I am confident that he who created the universe and sustains it daily will administer this Will and see that my wishes are carried out to his glory. He already knows all of my beloved, having created each one, and I am sure that he who began a good work within you will perform it until I come to receive you unto myself.

B. What powers do I give my executor? He, the Source of all power, is able to do exceeding abundantly above all that you could ask or think, infinitely beyond your highest prayers, desires, thoughts, or hopes. He can accomplish what he will.

[Page One of My Will]

ARTICLE III.

BURIAL INSTRUCTIONS

I prefer that my burial be accomplished without any undue cost or inconvenience to anyone. Please do not spend a large sum for a tomb, for I will only use it for three days. If anyone should offer a tomb, I agree to return it after the weekend.

ARTICLE IV.

NOMINATION OF GUARDIAN

I hereby nominate and appoint as guardian of my beloved, the Comforter, the Spirit of Truth. I will not leave my beloved comfortless. The Comforter will lead them into all truth. He will teach them all things and bring all things to their remembrance, whatsoever I have said (John 14:16–18, 26).

ARTICLE V.

FORGIVENESS OF DEBTS

I do hereby forgive all who believe in me (my "beloved"), and I instruct my executor to cancel, blot out, and remove all their sins, as far as the east is from the west, and to put them behind his back and remember them no more. I, who have never known sin, have been made sin for them, and I direct that my righteousness, the righteousness which is of God by faith, to be imputed to them. I direct that the beloved be made white as snow and be granted a complete pardon for their sins.

ARTICLE VI.

SPECIFIC LEGACIES

A. I have not spent my brief time on earth in search of possessions that rust corrupts or moths destroy or thieves break in and steal. Instead I have relied on my father to meet my needs, and he has faithfully done so.

[Page Two of My Will]

B. My sole earthly possession is my robe. I make no provision for its disposition, because before the cock crows, it will be taken from me, leaving me naked and destitute, as I came into this world.

C. Silver and gold have I none, but from my storehouse of eternal riches in glory that my father has given me, I leave to each of my beloved, on this evening before I depart earth, the following gifts, all of which are guaranteed brand new:

1. A New Home. I am going to prepare a place for my beloved, I will return and receive them unto myself, so that they may live forever where I am (John 14:3; 17:24).

2. A New Promise. If my beloved ask for anything in my name, I will do it. I promise (John 15:7).

3. A New Life. Because I live, my beloved shall live also, eternally with me (John 14:19).

4. A New Family. All who believe in me are my family, "that they may all be one" (John 17:21).

5. A New Peace. "Peace I leave with you; my peace I give you" (John 14:27 NIV). Don't let your heart be troubled.

6. A New Joy. These things I have spoken unto my beloved that my joy will remain, and that their joy might be full—the joy that no man will take from them (John 15:11; 16:22).

7. A New Power. My beloved are hereby empowered to do greater works than I have done (John 14:12).

ARTICLE VII.

STATE OF MIND

At the time that I make this will, I am of sound mind. My head is clear. I know what I am doing. I am fully aware that I will die tomorrow.

I voluntarily will make myself a sacrifice. I will not accept wine as a sedative. Nor will I run from the task set before me. Nor will I call 10,000 angels to deliver me.

For the joy that is set before me, I will endure the cross, for you—voluntarily. I will endure every rejection, every sorrow, every thorn, every curse, every lie, every beating, every slash, every nail, every sword, every sin—for you.

[Page Three of My Will]

IN WITNESS WHEREOF, I, the undersigned, have set my hand on this day before my death. This will is sealed, with my blood.

Signed by:
JESUS CHRIST
aka
The Savior,
The Good Shepherd,
The Lamb of God,
The Way, the Truth, and the Life,
Wonderful Counselor,
Son of God,
The Prince of Peace,
The Cornerstone,
Jehovah,
El Shaddai Adonai,
The Resurrection and the Life,
The Alpha and the Omega,
The Beginning and the End,
The Messiah

Witnesses: This will was witnessed personally by the disciples of Jesus. John wrote, "I am that disciple! I saw these events and have recorded them here. And we all know that my account of these things is accurate" (John 21:24).

Historical Note: The testator died in A.D. 30 in Jerusalem outside the city gates on the day after this nuncupative will was executed. The precise cause of death is unclear, but when I asked that question of a coroner, he suggested that death by crucifixion is usually due to one or more of the following mechanisms: (1) suspension of body by the extremities, causing respiratory fatigue and failure with resultant postural asphyxia and slow heart failure; (2) exposure to the elements; (3) dehydration; and (4) loss of blood. However, others believe the testator died of a broken heart.[1]

Notice to all beneficiaries, herein called his beloved: The executor of this will, the everlasting Father, is prepared to make immediate distribution to all of the beloved named herein. Those claiming status "in the beloved" are hereby declared to be heirs of Jesus and may begin to appropriate all of their rights and privileges as heirs immediately. The procedure for realizing benefits is "to ask whatever you will in his name." No limitations are placed either in amount or frequency. His estate is large enough to honor all requests. And he guarantees to honor each one.

Notice to hearers of this will who are not included as beneficiaries: Before he died, Jesus Christ expressed a fervent desire that no one be excluded as a beneficiary under his will. He said that whosoever believes in him should be included in the beloved. Hence the class of beneficiaries under his will is still open.

[1]Special thanks to Jay Barnhart, forensic pathologist and associate medical examiner in Dade County, Miami, Florida.

# 27

# Handle with Care

I had just come home from work one afternoon as Marabel was preparing dinner when I noticed a package of chicken on the counter.

"Want me to cut up the chicken for you?"

"No. It's frozen solid."

"That's no problem," I told her, and with that I picked up a long knife to begin surgery.

Well, in the process of cutting (or trying to cut up) a frozen chicken, I made several important discoveries that will live long past me. First of all, long knives aren't necessarily the best utensils for cutting frozen chickens, or frozen anythings! Secondly, it's a lot easier to cut a cooked chicken than a raw chicken. Finally, chickens are tough birds, and frozen chickens are *very* tough birds.

After bending one knife and doing minor damage to the countertop, I wasn't discouraged. I thought, "Remember, Charlie, this is just a chicken. A two-pound chicken, born to be a McNugget. You can do it!"

I went to heavier artillery—a cleaver. I took a hammer to hit the cleaver. As I tackled the leg/thigh joint, I thought, "This is one tough chicken—probably an All-Pro Guard in the National Chicken League! The leg joint alone could support a sixty-five pound chicken!"

A moment later the cleaver missed. Missed the chicken, that is, but not my hand. I had quite a mess on my hands. I spent the evening getting emergency medical attention, and we never did get back to that chicken!

For the next week, I discovered that without the use of my hand I was severely restricted in my activities. I was literally "handicapped."

One night as I rebandaged my hand, I looked at my hands and thought, "You guys are a remarkable team, especially when you're both healthy! I hadn't thought much about you before, but I really appreciate you now!"

I asked myself, "Self, what is a hand anyway?" According to Webster, a hand is described as "the terminal part of the arm when, as in man and the apes, it is specially modified as a grasping organ. Part serving the function of or like a hand as the foot of an ape, the chela of a crustacean."

What? Come on, Webster, you can do better than that, can't you? Something better than "the terminal part of the arm, as in man and the apes"?!

Then I thought, maybe it's easier to describe what a hand *does* than what it *is*. What can a hand do? I looked down at my hands.

With these hands, I can play a piano. I can hold a pencil, shake a hand, slap a volleyball, make a fist, dial a telephone, wipe a table, grip a baseball, juggle, strum a guitar, thread a needle, caress a child, pick up a coin, recognize braille, and carry water without spilling.

A hand can also turn to accommodate its master. A hand is an indispensable part of the human body. It's Action Central, where things happen.

I wondered what it was like years ago when Jesus was arrested. I thought about his hands—those strong, loving hands. I thought how many ways he had used them for good. How important were those hands! Yet when he was arrested, he was probably booked like an ordinary criminal, and fingerprinted as well.

### The Hands of Jesus

*Building hands.* As a carpenter, Jesus' rugged hands held a saw and a hammer and nails. His were the hands of a craftsman.

*Providing hands.* When 5,000 men had nothing to eat, Jesus made do with what they had—five rolls and two fish. He blessed the mini-meal, then with those wonderful hands, he broke the rolls, again and again, until all were fed.

*Indicting hands.* Jesus was teaching at the temple when the Jewish leaders brought an adulteress to him and asked, "This woman was

| PERSONAL IDENTIFICATION | | | | |
|---|---|---|---|---|

Name *Jesus Christ*

| No. | F.B.I. No. | Class. | | |
|---|---|---|---|---|
| | B.C.I. No. | Ref. | | |

Impressions taken by *A. K. Pierce*, B.R.P.D.

| Date | | By | | |
|---|---|---|---|---|

**Right Hand**

| 1. Right Thumb | 2. R. Fore Finger | 3. R. Middle Finger | 4. R. Ring Finger | 5. R. Little Finger |
|---|---|---|---|---|
| | | | | |

**Left Hand**

| 6. Left Thumb | 7. L. Fore Finger | 8. L. Middle Finger | 9. L. Ring Finger | 10. L. Little Finger |
|---|---|---|---|---|
| | | | | |

| Left Hand Plain Impressions Taken Simultaneously | | Right Hand Plain Impressions Taken Simultaneously | |
|---|---|---|---|
| Left Hand-Four Fingers | L. Thumb | R. Thumb | Right Hand-Four Fingers |
| | | | |

*Please Do Not Fold This Card*

caught in the very act of adultery. Moses' law says to kill her. What about it?"

Jesus said, "All right, hurl the stones at her until she dies. But only he who never sinned may throw the first!" (John 8:4–7). Then with his finger he began writing in the sand. What he wrote, we don't know. Maybe it was her lover's name or maybe the names of community leaders who'd been with her. In any event, when Jesus looked up, they were all gone, and he said to her, "Where are your accusers? Didn't even one of them condemn you? Neither do I" (John 8:10–11).

*Healing hands.* Mighty works were also performed by those hands. The touch of the Master's hands brought healing to the incurable. For example:

- A paralyzed woman when he put his hands on her (Luke 13:13)
- Peter's deathly sick mother-in-law when he touched her hand (Matt. 8:15)
- Jairus's dead daughter when Jesus took her by the hand and raised her to life (Mark 5:41–42)

- The high priest's servant, whose ear Peter had cut off, when Jesus touched the place where the man's ear had been and restored it whole (Luke 22:51)

*Blessing hands.* He put his hands on little children and blessed them. How he loved the little children! (Mark 10:16).

*Saving hands.* When Peter tried walking on water and started to sink, Jesus reached out his hand and caught him (Matt. 14:31).

*Serving hands.* At the Last Supper, Jesus got up from the table and washed his disciples' feet, wiping them with a towel (John 13:4–5). Then he took the cup and broke bread, telling them to eat and drink "in remembrance of me" (Luke 22:17–19).

*Suffering hands.* Jesus was forced to carry his own cross with his hands (Matt. 27:32).

*Bleeding hands.* Jesus' hands were then nailed to the cross, nails piercing those loving hands. Spikes punctured those loving hands. Healing hands became bleeding hands. Jesus said, "I love you this much" and spread out his arms and died.

*Protecting hands.* Those protecting hands of Jesus are still in use. Before his death, he promised that all believers would be kept secure: "No one can snatch them out of my hand" (John 10:28 NIV).

You're in good hands with Jesus.

# 28

# Good Morning, Jerusalem

For many, Sunday morning is a once-a-week chance to sleep in. But on one Sunday morning, about A.D. 30, three women were very glad they didn't. Rising early, they went to Jesus' tomb with spices, intending to properly prepare his body for burial.

On that morning, there was an earthquake that knocked the heavy stone from the entry to the tomb. When the women reached the tomb, it was both open and empty, and an angel announced Jesus' resurrection.

The women ran to tell the disciples the news, and Peter and John ran back to see for themselves. Yes, the body was gone.

The news spread quickly through the city. Priests bribed the guards to say that the body was stolen. But then Jesus began to appear to his disciples—on the road and in the upper room, even preaching to large groups as he had before. Jesus was indeed risen from the dead, and the world would never be the same.

How might the Jerusalem morning show have covered that history-making morning?

Good Morning Jerusalem Show
Sunday Morning—6:00 A.M. Transcript

IRVING: Good morning, this is Irving R. Mudd.

IDA: And this is Ida Rather. Welcome to the Good Morning Jerusalem Show, bringing you the first news of the day, brought to you by WJNN, the Jerusalem News Network. When you want to be there, but can't, we already are. WJNN brings you all the news you care to hear, and then some. Now here's Irving with this morning's news.

Morning News

IRVING: Well, the big story this morning is the violent earthquake that shook Jerusalem an hour ago. The first jolt was felt at the Garden Cemetery at dawn, according to three women who stopped by the station. They just happened to be at the cemetery when it started to quake. The reporter at our city desk said, "They didn't look like waitresses heading to work at the Zion Pancake House. But then why were they in a graveyard early in the morning?!"

The quake has leveled several homes in Golgotha Estates. The Gethsemane Garden Apartment Building has collapsed, leaving dozens trapped beneath the rubble. Rescue teams have rushed to the devastated areas, and off-duty officers are being called in.

The quake has registered a VI.VIII on the Roman Scale. Shock waves have been reported throughout the city and as far away as Jericho.

The quake comes but three days after the big jolt to Jerusalem last Friday during the unprecedented three-hour noon blackout. The Friday quake and blackout happened coincidentally during the crucifixions of Jesus of Nazareth and two notorious criminals at Golgotha, where hundreds had gathered to watch the macabre event. Some local leaders have attached special significance to this happenstance.

The epicenter of this morning's quake seems to be in that Garden Tomb area where the three women happened to be earlier this morning. Graves are reportedly split open. Police advise residents to stay away from that area.

Traffic Report

IDA: We now bring you our first traffic report of the morning through the courtesy of Molly's Gourmet Matzohs at Caleb and Western. When you think of matzohs, think of Molly.

The Jerusalem PD has issued a special traffic bulletin—"Unless your job this morning is vital for life or rescue, the two words for you are 'Forget it!'"

The Jerusalem Bypass is closed due to fallen debris on the road. The Damascus Gate is closed and there's a long backup at Herod's Gate. So drive carefully and keep those saddle straps snug. Remember, saddle straps save lives. Now this. . . .

Sports

IRVING: In sports yesterday, Tullian won the 25K Dead Sea Marathon from Jerusalem.

The Passover Stakes was run yesterday at Palestine Downs. The feature race was won by Temple Terror, paying 13.40, 8.20, and 3.50 denarii.

Today's big chariot race, the Jerusalem Grand Prix, has been canceled due to road conditions.

Special Bulletin

IDA: We interrupt our regular news segment to bring you this special bulletin. Jesus Christ is reported to be alive. Dead on Friday, alive on Sunday?! This report came from the same three women who reported the earthquake early this morning. These eyewitnesses claim they just talked with him outside his tomb. We now switch you to the garden tomb to our reporter Sara Sawyer.

SARA: Yes, Ida, I have with me Mary Magdalene, who earlier today visited our studio to file the first quake report.

MARY M.: My friend Salome and I both saw him. He's alive! He's the same person. He's different—you know, like glorified, shining, but he's Jesus. I know his voice. He knew my name. He's alive!

SARA: Wow, what a story! Back to you, Ida.

# Jerusalem *News* Network

IDA: Oh, here's a call on our hotline. Simon Peter, one of Jesus' followers who has been in hiding. Good morning, Simon.

PETER: Good morning, Ida. First of all, I've just changed my name, or rather he changed it. My new name is Rock, but my friends call me Rocky.

IDA: Rocky, you said you saw Jesus. Sure you did, but how do we know that your jolly little band didn't steal his body?

PETER: No, I saw him, really. Jesus is alive.

IDA: Right. Thank you, Rocky.

IRVING: Let's take some calls. My producer says that the board is jammed. WJNN.

MATTHEW: This is Matthew, the former tax collector. I'm sure you remember me.

IRVING: How could I forget the time you foreclosed on my house!

MATTHEW: Well, sorry about that. That was the old Matthew. I just saw Jesus this morning. He had a fish sandwich with a few . . .

IRVING: Oops! Matthew, sorry, gotta run. WJNN.

MARY: Yes. This is Mary, Jesus' mother. My son is alive again! Before Jesus was born, an angel told me that this would happen and now I understand, and when . . .

IRVING: Sorry, Mary, gotta go. WJNN.

ANTHONY: This is Anthony. I was the officer in charge of the crucifixion of Jesus on Friday.

IRVING: OK, thank goodness, officer, we finally got a lucid caller. Can we talk? You were on the scene when Jesus was killed last Friday, is that right? It's pretty important for us to determine if he actually died. We've been getting calls saying the guy's alive. So, did Jesus really die on Friday? Are you sure he was dead?

ANTHONY: I am dead sure of it, if you'll pardon the pun. Jesus was dead on Friday. No man could survive what he went through. But I'll tell you something else. This man was the Son of God.

IRVING: Well if he was dead on Friday, how can he be alive on Sunday? And why do you say he's the Son of God?

ANTHONY: I just saw Jesus alive, going into an upper room at Bethany. I said, "My Lord," and then he hugged me and he called me "Brother Anthony!" Can't figure how he knew my name! Then he went into the upper room, and get this—he went right through a closed door! This man is the Son of God.

# Jerusalem *News* Network

IRVING: Thank you, officer, gotta run. WJNN.

IDA: Rachel, check that out will you? How are we doing with calls? Let me see my messages. Wow, what a pile. All reporting Jesus sightings. And they aren't flakes either. Here's Joseph of Arimathea (big bucks guy), Zacchaeus (little guy, big bucks), Nicodemus (big time clout), Bartimaeus (former blind guy), Simon (former leper), some Samaritan woman, Lazarus (former dead guy), several kids. Must be over five hundred here. Here's a call that says that Jesus is speaking to a crowd outside of Bethany right now. Unbelievable!

IRVING: Well, we'll now be signing off. Stay tuned to Wheel of Chariots. For me, I'm headed to Bethany to consider the source for myself. This is Irving R. Mudd.

IDA: And this is Ida Rather. Good morning, Jerusalem.

# Jerusalem *News* Network

# 29

# Jesus Is My Advocate

It all started over twenty-five years ago when he represented me in a capital case where I was facing the death penalty.

The righteous Judge read out the charges against me in open court in a loud voice.

I looked around for a jury of my peers. There was none.

There was no chance for any private sidebar conversation.

It was brutally embarrassing as charges were read against me and caused me to recall my prior wrongs.

The evidence was overwhelmingly against me. I was accused of multiple charges that filled books and books—a library full.

There was no chance of getting out on a technicality. My DNA was a perfect match. It was me.

There was no way for me to pay the fines. There was no way to plea-bargain.

I told the Judge I was without funds, without hope, without defense. I was dead to rights. Guilty on all counts.

I threw myself on the mercy of the court and pled guilty as charged.

Then something remarkable happened. The Public Defender suddenly appeared by my side. My Lawyer took my punishment. My

Advocate became my Atonement. He died and I walked. He satisfied my sentence. I was acquitted. Forgiven.

The Judge declared me not guilty. No, even better, declared me innocent and spotless. (I knew better and so did he. But he accepted my Advocate.)

The decision was made by the Judge who looked right through me. But instead of looking at my sweaty palms, the Judge looked at my Advocate's pierced palms.

I hope you get to know my Lawyer. He's never lost a case. He's never let me down. He never leaves me. He'll never leave you either.

And when your case is all over, you can keep him on retainer, but he won't send you a bill.

He's a great one to have representing you since his father's the Judge.

# Conclusion

Finishing is better than starting!
King Solomon
Ecclesiastes 7:8

How do you close a book about Jesus? Or *can* you close the book on Jesus?

I can't.

Jesus' life can't be dismissed simply as "Jesus Christ A.D. 1–30."

His epitaph can't be written because there is no tombstone. A grave, yes, but an empty one. Unoccupied.

Who is Jesus anyway? Who is this one-of-a-kind being who walked our streets?

Some called him the Enigma Man. Superman. All-Purpose Man. Superstar. A Man for All Seasons.

One prophet called him wonderful Counselor, mighty God, everlasting Father, Prince of Peace, and Immanuel.

He called himself the Son of God, Son of Man, Love, Truth, Life, Messiah, Good Shepherd, and Lamb of God.

Saint John calls him King of Kings and Lord of Lords.

He is all of the above.

He's the One who left the grave before the mourners arrived to grieve.

He's the One who's no longer with us, but yet he is.

He's the One for whom death held no power.

He's the One who turned a funeral into a homecoming.

He's the One who coined a new word: resurrection.

He's the One who returned his borrowed tomb after a weekend.

He's the One who said, "It is finished," while taking his last breath, with confidence that his father would raise him up after three days.

In the face of his spotless, compassionate life, there were those who tried to kill him, bury him, and get on with other business. But could they?

Pilate couldn't with his order of execution.

The soldiers couldn't with nails.

The temple couldn't with guards.

The guards couldn't with a stone.

Death couldn't hold him.

Good Friday is over. Easter celebrates his new life, and ours.

Julia Howe, composer of the "Battle Hymn of the Republic," summed up the life of Jesus this way:

In the beauty of the lilies, Christ was born across the sea,
With a glory in his bosom that transfigures you and me;
As he died to make men holy, let us live to make men free,
While God is marching on.
Glory! Glory! Hallelujah. Our God is marching on.

So where is Jesus now?

For sure he walked our streets. For sure he died. For sure he's not in that tomb.

He lives, he lives.

Where two or three are gathered in his name, he is there.

In the valley of the shadow of death, he is there.

When you go through deep waters, he is there.

When you go through fiery trials, he is there.

When you reach the end of the age, he'll be there waiting with arms open wide.

John, the eyewitness journalist, trying to wrap up his biography of Jesus, expressed his frustration at trying to finish his task—of the finite trying to capture the infinite. Finally he said, "If all the other events in Jesus' life were written, the world could hardly contain the books!" (John 21:25).

Those books are still being written. This is but one. Many others will follow until the time that he returns. Then our books will be closed, and his Book of Life will be opened.

And we shall behold him.